W. E. B. DU BOIS: A BIOGRAPHY

W. E. B. Du Bois

A BIOGRAPHY

by **VIRGINIA HAMILTON**
Illustrated with Photographs

THOMAS Y. CROWELL · NEW YORK

ACKNOWLEDGMENTS

Grateful and sincere acknowledgment is made to Dr. Herbert Aptheker for his critical reading of, and detailed commentary on, the original manuscript; for his continued interest and selfless cooperation.

In addition, we wish to thank the organizations and individuals who supplied the photographs from their files for this book. Every effort has been made to trace the ownership of all copyrighted material, and in the event of any question arising as to the use of any selections, we will, while expressing regret for any errors we may have made, be glad to make the necessary corrections in future editions of this book.

Designed by CAROLE FERN HALPERT

Manufactured in the United States of America
L.C. Card 70-175106
ISBN 0-690-87256-9
4 5 6 7 8 9 10

In memory of Kenneth Hamilton, Sr.
For Those Who Labor

As, then, a citizen of the world as well as of the United States of America, I claim the right to know and think and tell the truth as I see it. I believe in Socialism as well as Democracy. I believe in Communism wherever and whenever men are wise and good enough to achieve it; but I do not believe that all nations will achieve it in the same way or at the same time. I despise men and nations which judge human beings by their color, religious beliefs or income. I believe in free enterprise among free men and individual initiative under physical, biological and social law. I hate War.

—W. E. B. DU BOIS, 1952
In Battle for Peace

CHAPTER 1

DR. WILLIAM EDward Burghardt Du Bois lay dying in the city of Accra, Ghana, on the coast of West Africa. He was the black man who, with obvious love, had called all black people "my people." The age-old fight for equality waged by blacks everywhere had been "his" battle for more than half a century, and winning it would have been the greatest achievement of his life. For years William Du Bois had led "his" people in their protest struggle for liberty; now he lay dying far away from America, the country of his birth.

Life flickered and flamed, then faltered, in the ninety-five-year-old Dr. Du Bois. He had moments of consciousness throughout the solemn evening, and he was told that all was well in America. Back home it was the eve of a monumental gathering. Blacks and whites by the thousands were preparing to march on Washington, D.C., the next day. Every step they took would lead them closer to the freedom of which the Doctor had dreamed. Every song they sang would speak of justice, which he had worked so hard to make a reality.

Twenty minutes before midnight, on August 27, 1963, Dr. W. E. B. Du Bois died. The following day nearly half a million Americans carried out the largest protest demonstration ever seen in the United States. In the songs and slogans of the thousands on the move was the courageous spirit for which the Doctor had strived in the past.

William Du Bois had been a scholar and teacher of great depth and talent. As a poet and often a prophet, he could have spent his life comfortably in isolated, intellectual peace. He might easily have become the right sort of "Negro" fashionable white people were pleased to have live in their upper-class neighborhoods. Instead he chose to lead the struggle for equal rights for all those who labor. Had he lived to walk with the many thousands marching on Washington in 1963, he might have recalled words of the gallant poem he wrote in the hard times of 1899:

> *I am the smoke king,*
> *I am black.*
> *I am swinging in the sky.*
> *I am ringing worlds on high:*
> *I am the thought of the throbbing mills,*
> *I am the soul of the soul toil kills,*
> *I am the ripple of trading rills,*
>
> *Up I'm curling from the sod,*
> *I am whirling home to God.*

I am the smoke king,
I am black.[1]

William Edward Burghardt Du Bois, in 1868, had the good fortune to be born into an astonishing clan of black people who had come to America's east coast two hundred years before his birth:

My grandfather's grandmother was seized by an evil Dutch trader two centuries ago; and coming to the valleys of the Hudson and Housatonic, black, little, and lithe, she shivered and shrank in the harsh north winds, looked longingly at the hills, and often crooned a heathen melody to the child between her knees, thus:

Do bana co-ba, ge-ne me, ge-ne me!
Do bana co-ba, ge-ne me, ge-ne me!
Ben d'nu-li, nu-li ben d'le.

The child sang it to his children and they to their children's children, and so two hundred years it has travelled down to us and we sing it to our children, knowing as little as our fathers what its words may mean, but knowing well the meaning of its music.[2]

Coenraet Borghardt, or Burghardt, was the Dutch slave trader who brought to the Hudson valley the slave child, Tom Burghardt. Tom had been born in West Africa about 1730. Seized by the white Coenraet Borghardt, he came east eventually with the Borghardt family to the virgin and forbidding wilderness of Berkshire County, Massachusetts. There Tom grew up and married a black African of the Bantu tribe. She may have been the African woman who brought with her from her homeland the haunting song "Do bana co-ba," which would one day be known by generations of black Burghardts.

Tom Burghardt became a private in the Revolutionary War and, with his family, was no longer regarded as a slave. Later on, the Massachusetts Bill of Rights of 1780 set all Massachusetts slaves free.

Before Tom died in 1787 he had sired seven sons, the most important of whom was Jack. For Jack, in turn, also had a large family. One of his sons, Othello, was William Burghardt Du Bois' grandfather.

Born in 1781, Othello Burghardt grew up to settle on the South Egremont Plain near Great Barrington, Massachusetts. With his brothers, Ira and Harlow, and his sister Lucinda, he took up farming and soon owned a small farm adjoining those of his brothers and sister. At the age of twenty Othello married a tall Dutch-African woman named Sarah Lampman, and they had ten children. A daughter, Mary, born to them in 1831, was the mother of William Burghardt Du Bois.

The farms the black Burghardt clan owned were never quite big enough to support the huge families born on them. The clan slowly gave up tilling the land, and a few joined the ranks of the adventuresome heading west. Those who remained on Egremont Plain became houseworkers or day laborers in the towns. Mary Burghardt found work as a servant in homes owned by whites in Great Barrington. She was a soft-spoken, bronze-skinned woman whose quiet manner gave no hint of her strong Burghardt will.

Mary had an unhappy love affair with a cousin, after which the cousin went away to California. She then met Alfred Du Bois and at once fell in love with him.

Alfred Du Bois was something of a dreamer. He came to the Berkshire valley and Great Barrington in 1867. A small man, just noticeably black, he had yellow skin and curly hair. He resembled his father, Alexander Du Bois, and his white grandfather, James Du Bois.

Alfred's grandfather, Dr. James Du Bois, had been a prosperous plantation owner in the Bahama Islands. Never marrying, James Du Bois had two sons by one of his black slaves. The sons were Alexander, born in 1803, and John, born some time later. Both boys looked white, and for this reason Dr. James Du Bois thought he could safely bring them to the northern United States. He placed Alexander in the private Cheshire School in Connecticut and often visited him there.

On one such visit James Du Bois died of a stroke. He left no will, and his considerable estate went to a cousin. Immediately the education of John and Alexander Du Bois as gentlemen ended. The cousin took both boys out of school, cut them off without any money, and farmed them out as apprentices. In this way, all relations with the white Du Bois family ended.

No one knows what sort of apprentice John Du Bois became; however, Alexander Du Bois became an apprentice to a shoemaker and grew into a rebel. He had started out with a fine education, and he was shocked at the sudden, awful change in his life. Because of his father's cousin, he was now classed as "Negro." The "Negro" didn't so much disturb him as did the contempt with which whites treated him and the harshness to which all "Negroes" were subjected.

Alexander Du Bois became outspoken against race prejudice, but he took his bitter disinheritance without a fight. Too proud, perhaps, to make a plea for his father's wealth, he would not stoop to fight with thieving cousins. For the rest of his life Alexander wore his telltale blackness proudly. And yet, a deep inner rage kept him always on the move, seething, seeking and never quite finding what he was looking for. In Haiti, on one of his wild searches for his luck, he got married, and soon Alfred Du Bois was born.

In all, Alexander Du Bois married three times and was the father of four children. He became a forceful and forbidding father, but secretly he wrote poetry. Alexander was especially fond of his youngest son, Alfred, who was most like him. However, he was much too strict with him, and Alfred ran away. He became a wanderer and ended up in the valleys of the Housatonic and Hudson rivers. There he found the shy brown woman Mary, a charming member of the clannish Burghardt family.

Alfred Du Bois was forty-two years old when he and Mary ran away to marry in 1867. Alfred hadn't been married before. One year later, Alfred and Mary's son, William Edward Burghardt Du Bois, was born in Great Barrington.

In William's blood there would be forever a temperamental strain of French and a bitter ooze of Dutch slavers. In 1868, the year of William's birth, former slaves voted for the first time in their lives. The Emancipation Proclamation had begun their liberation only five years before. Black people were beginning to take part in government in great numbers, and black delegates voted new and democratic constitutions everywhere in the South. This period of Reconstruction (1867–1877) was a time of new hope for black people. Into this significant time William Burghardt Du Bois was born in a house beside the "golden" Housatonic River.

As it still is, Great Barrington was a small valley town in the southwestern corner of Massachusetts. The Housatonic River moved slowly through the town, taking its name from the village of Housatonic not ten miles north of Great Barrington.

Surrounding Great Barrington were the Berkshire Hills, which closed out the rest of the world. The main street of Great Barrington was lined with elm trees. The foothills were covered with white pine trees and orchards. Above these were rocks and caves, magnificent in shape and size.

There were as few as fifty blacks in this town of five thousand people. The Burghardt family was among the oldest citizenry of the Berkshire valley. William Burghardt Du Bois was born in a house owned by a black man from South Carolina named Jefferson McKinley. McKinley had recently settled in the Berkshires; he wore golden earrings and was able to put himself into religious trances. His wood-frame clapboarded house, situated at the end of a long lane, had five rooms, a small porch, and a front yard full of roses. But always restless, Alfred soon left the house to start a new life in Connecticut, where he hoped to build a home for Mary and William.

The strict Burghardt family never cared much for Alfred Du Bois. When he arrived in Great Barrington, they found him "too good-looking, too white." As far as they knew, he had no job and few prospects of any. They had never heard of this Du Bois family from New York, and they feuded with Alfred and Mary until the birth of William.

The entire town of Great Barrington seemed to be concerned with William. The whites were curious to find out whether the hair on the head of such a white-looking baby would curl, and all of the Burghardts made an outlandish fuss over him. A year after he was born Alfred Du Bois left Great Barrington for good. He wrote Mary that she and the baby should join him within a few months, but Mary had not often been away from her hometown. The Burghardt clan hated to have her and the dearly loved baby leave them. Finally, it happened that Mary didn't leave. Alfred Du Bois didn't return to her and his son. And William Du Bois never saw his father. William had to live without a father, but in the large and faithful Burghardt clan his childhood was a happy one.

Soon after Alfred's departure William and his mother moved from the McKinley house to grandfather Othello Burghardt's farm home on South Egremont Plain. The small, old-fashioned house was a delightful place for a child. William and his mother shared its pleasures for five years, until grandfather Othello died. With Othello's wife, grandmother Sally, and William, Mary Du Bois moved back to town and to rooms over stables on a tract of land called the Sumner estate. William called his new home simply "upstairs," and he loved it. There was a yard, wide and full of shrubbery, to play in. There was a sweet, bubbling brook to wade in.

Opposite the front gate of the estate was a lane leading down to the public school grounds. From the age of five to the age of sixteen, William went to school down the lane and into the broad yard with one wood and one brick building. It was during these years spent in the "upstairs" and in school that William grew to know his world and to judge it for the pleasant but narrow place it was.

William and his mother were close to poverty most of the time, but he was never hungry, nor made to feel different from other children. Even though there were social classes in Great Barrington, the families with money made no display of it. And there was no one in the town who could be called wealthy. However, the glint and sparkle of wealth could be seen each day. The Housatonic River flowing through Great Barrington was "golden" in color because the paper and woolen mills emptied their wastes into it. The mill owners had the real gold in money. Still, William and all of Great Barrington could have the shimmering yellow river. But it was polluted even then.

William came to accept the social situation in his town and managed to fit himself into it. Most of the people he saw each day were middle-class farmers, merchants, and skilled workers. The unskilled laborers were mainly Irish and German mill workers. They lived on the opposite side of the river from William and close to the Catholic church. Or they lived in the slums surrounding the woolen mills. William was quick to learn a middle-class point of view and was able to put everyone in his proper place. From the vantage of his polite New England upbringing, he looked down on the mill workers. And beyond the security of the strong Burghardt clan he made what friends he needed among the middle class and near-rich.

The black people in Great Barrington were so few in number, they couldn't have been thought of as a class. Most belonged to strict clans like the Burghardt family, held tightly together through family history and the color of their skin. When one of the Burghardt cousins brought home a white wife one day, the family objected to her because they didn't know who her family was or how the cousin would support her. Her white skin neither impressed nor disturbed them.

The times when William needed shoes or school-books, Burghardt uncles or aunts supplied the money. Occasionally gifts came from white families who had known and respected the Burghardts all of their lives.

In Great Barrington there was nothing that could have been called a social life. Group events centered around the town's churches, which were all white-owned. The black people came together easily according to their clan or family traditions and freely took part in the social life of the churches.

When grandmother Sally Burghardt died in 1877, five years after the death of grandfather Othello, William and his mother moved to Railroad Street, next to the station. Soon afterward his mother had a stroke, which left her with a paralyzed leg and withered hand. But life for William continued much the same as it had been before. He had plenty to eat; he went to school. Relatives did most of what had to be done, and neighbors were generous and always willing to help. Mary Du Bois worked when she was able. At night William went to meet his mother after work and was never left home alone.

His relations with adults and children in Great Barrington were rather ordinary and usually pleasant. William sometimes was the leader of a group of boys who made great commotions but were never really very tough or bad. Boys his age weren't allowed to fool around the streets but were made to go to bed early. Like the others, William didn't mind this particularly, since the daytime life of the town was close to paradise. In summer the boys could swim the river and climb the hills. In winter the same hills were snow-king mountains, fine for sledding. Always there were dark, forbidding caves to explore and great gray rocks to rest upon.

William took part in the normal life of the town youths—Sunday school picnics, skating at the rink, and sledding parties. He knew well the homes of most of his schoolmates; he played with the boys and he ate with them. But gradually he understood that he wasn't the same as other children. At first he thought that his quickness in school had somehow set him apart. Then he noticed that his appearance, his brown skin and kinky hair, could quite suddenly cause him to become the center of attention. There were always some people who looked at him as if being brown were a stroke of bad luck; a few even looked at him contemptuously, as though his color were a criminal offense.

This introduction into the world of color prejudice was painful for William until his mother assured him that prejudice did not exist. Getting on in life, she told William, was a matter of ability and hard work. William had little reason to doubt her, for he was smart in everything, and no one ever thought of separating him from the other boys. It was he who invented the games they played. Among the best students in his school, he was usually the youngest of his class because he skipped so many grades.

So it was that William grew out of feelings of rejection and was drawn into believing that he was intended for some higher goal in life. This dream was particularly helpful when it came to his relationship with girls.

In Great Barrington teen-age boys were never supposed to show any regard for girls. Once in a while girls were allowed to participate in some games the boys played, and William would play with them at these times. But the girls treated him differently if he chanced to meet them in public, or when strangers or summer vacationers were watching. The summer people stared at him and obviously didn't approve of this "colored" child having contact with white children. The girls would snub him at these times, and William would become furious. He would disappear into the hills, where he would sit for hours like some brooding giant watching the crawling movement of the world below. Here his dreams were as lofty as the hills, and he vowed to be the best in everything, the smartest in school.

William was raised knowing that regular schooling was a proper part of life. It was unusual for a black family in the nineteenth century to have attended school for generations the way his family had. All of

William's relatives could read and write. And he himself avidly studied reading, writing, spelling, arithmetic,
grammar, geography, and history.

He worked part-time splitting kindling and mowing
lawns, but his first regular job came when he entered
high school. William found employment in the millinery
shop of a Madame L'Hommedieu, filling the stove with
coal. From that time on and throughout high school,
William worked after school and on Saturdays selling
newspapers, distributing tea sent up from the A & P
stores based in New York, and acting as the local correspondent for a few months for the *Springfield Republican.* This newspaper job came about through Johnny
Morgan, a man of Welsh descent who ran the town's
bookshop. William had become fascinated by the
periodicals and books in Johnny Morgan's store.
Morgan was sympathetic to the young Du Bois and
allowed him to look into the books and magazines. It
had been Morgan who arranged for William to become
a correspondent.

William held many odd jobs through these years, but
the work open to black youths remained limited and
limiting. There was day labor. There was farming. A
boy such as William could go into house service or
work in summer hotels. But for a young and ambitious
black youth with a good education there were few
opportunities.

William's high school principal was Frank Hosmer,
who years later became president of Oahu College in

Hawaii. Noting William's fine intelligence, Hosmer suggested that he take the college-preparatory course, which included algebra, geometry, Latin, and Greek. For such a curriculum a student was required to buy all of his own books. William knew that he and his mother couldn't afford to pay for the books, but probably through Hosmer's influence the mother of one of William's playmates, the wife of a mill owner, offered to furnish them. That was how William Du Bois became a high school student preparing for college. He suddenly found himself in an unusual position in the town, for going to college was virtually impossible for a poor boy whether black or white.

CHAPTER 2

WILLIAM DU BOIS attended high school on the same school grounds where he had begun his education. In his freshman year he was fully aware that he was gifted as a student. But again he began to experience tension and frustration from real and imaginary slights because of his color. In all of the years of his schooling there had been only one other black student, and there were no others in his high school of twenty-five students and two teachers.

The isolation from other black youths and the restraint of his New England upbringing caused William to center his concerns more and more within himself. He shied away from reaching out for friendship with other students and protected himself from insult by forcing those who wished to be his friends to seek him out. William was generally saved from painful rejection by white female students because, as we have seen, teen-age boys and girls in the town did little socializing. In high school there were no dances, hardly any coed discussions on the school grounds, and no fraternities or sororities.

Throughout these high school years William studied hard and well. In constant need of extra money to buy school supplies and also to help his mother, he sold the black weekly newspaper *New York Age,* besides working for Madame L'Hommedieu.

William graduated from high school in 1884, the only black student in his class of twelve. Each student gave a graduation oration, and William's talk centered on Wendell Phillips, one of America's great abolitionists and orators, who died that very year. New England at this time was deeply conscious of its abolitionist contribution in freeing four million black slaves, and William's fine speech was enthusiastically received. For the first time in his life he experienced warm applause and a small measure of fame.

The birth of freedom for blacks and for the whole of the South had begun just as William was born in 1868 and, regrettably, was coming to an end as he graduated from high school. By 1884, twenty years after the Civil War, Black Reconstruction and freedom in the South were over. Every southern state was now back in the hands of the very men who had made black people slaves. Yet, during Reconstruction, black men had been elected to state constitutional conventions to write the documents that would enable them to elect state legislatures (this took place before 1870, when blacks were given the vote by the Fifteenth Amendment). The blacks, in turn, had given the vote in new constitutions to their fellow white workers. Together the blacks and whites of the Reconstruction governments brought into existence for the first time free public schools for poor people of both races. They began legislation for the establishment of hospitals, instituted broad social welfare programs, and brought about the beginning of a wider distribution of land among the people. This period of Reconstruction was the only period in which true democracy ever existed in the South.

Tragically, this democratic rule was short-lived. For every freedom established during Black Reconstruction was overturned and abolished by the former slave-owners, who did not want to lose their vast source of cheap labor: the freed blacks. Thus the former slave-owners combined with northern industrial leaders to suppress the blacks. Black people soon lost their right to vote but managed to hold on to their schools, as poor as these were. By 1880 most of the southern states had returned to office leaders who designed programs that would deny freedom to blacks. The Ku Klux Klan, founded after the Civil War and outlawed by Congress in 1871, rose again to establish white supremacy. Wearing hoods and robes, poor whites were used by southern leaders to terrorize and often murder blacks.

William Du Bois was graduated into this situation in America at the age of sixteen. His own small problem was where to go to college, and, collecting college catalogs, he "blithely picked Harvard," he said, "because it was oldest and largest and most widely known."

The problem of what college to attend would not be one for William to solve for himself, however. His family and their white friends, after much discussion, decided that he was too young to go directly to college. Furthermore, the Great Barrington high school wasn't up to the standards of entrance requirements for a fine school like Harvard. William was advised to work and study one year more and then to enter college in the fall of 1885.

Frank Hosmer and others of the community's educators believed that skin color or lack of money shouldn't determine whether a youth such as William could attend college. Reverend C. C. Painter, whose son Charles had gone to school with William, had served in the Federal Indian Bureau. He believed that he knew the problems of the South, and he felt that the South was the place where William Du Bois should be educated. Reverend Painter was certain that William would find his work for the future in the South.

From the day of his birth William Du Bois had been the pride of the Burghardt family, and they deeply resented the idea of his going south to college. As northern blacks who had been free people during the Civil War, they naïvely believed that the North showed no prejudice toward blacks. But unknown to them, Great

Barrington was an isolated island of peace and tranquillity for black people. They knew nothing of the abject poverty and discrimination experienced by blacks in cities such as Boston, Philadelphia, and New York. However, they knew instinctively that the South would be a dangerous place for William, and the idea of sending him there for an education made them both fearful and furious. What most disturbed the black Burghardts was the fact that Great Barrington seemed not to want William. Instead of being given an opportunity for advancement right in his hometown or in the state, their gifted son was being quickly hustled away.

And what the Burghardt family felt was, of course, true. No one would deny that William was equal to any of the young whites who became clerks in the town's stores and teachers in its schools. But the idea of his living among them as a prominent member of the community and not as a poor black grateful for handouts hadn't occurred to any of the white elders of the town.

Reverend Painter offered William a scholarship to Fisk University, a black school in Nashville, Tennessee. The funds of the scholarship had been contributed by four Connecticut churches which Mr. Painter had formerly pastored.

William gladly accepted the scholarship. Although he had not given up the idea of someday going to Harvard, he was happy to go to Fisk, for it was the first step in the fulfillment of his dreams of college. He would be going into the South of slavery, of black people, and of "rebellion." And for the first time he would meet black students his own age, who had ambitions similar to his own.

For some time William had been aware of the isolation in which he lived in New England. Once, on a trip to visit his paternal grandfather, Alexander Du Bois, at Rocky Point on Narragansett Bay, he had attended a picnic by the sea, where ten thousand black people had gathered, he wrote, "in a gorgeous conglomerate of swaggering, self-assured men and beautiful girls."

And now, in the South, conservative southerners with active help from northern industrialists had swept back into political power. They detested the crusading New England teachers who had gone south during Reconstruction; they had hated Reconstruction, and they despised the freed Negroes. The white leaders' most successful method of stopping the political and social progress of black people was through violence. Negroes were being threatened with loss of jobs if they tried to vote. They were arrested and intimidated for any minor infraction of the law, and they were shot or lynched whenever they became too outspoken. By the end of the 1880s the conservatives had passed "Jim Crow"[1] laws which segregated blacks completely from whites.

President Ulysses S. Grant had signed a Civil Rights Act on March 1, 1875, which made discrimination illegal in hotels, theaters, and public carriers. But in October 1883 the United States Supreme Court declared the law unconstitutional.

Only seventeen, William saw discrimination such as this as merely a temporary setback for black people. In order for his race to take its rightful place in the South, he knew it would need trained leadership. And so it was with enthusiasm that he set out for Tennessee and Fisk in the fall of 1885. His mother had died just before he left Great Barrington. Now alone in the world, he grieved for her and kept close to his heart her great pride in the Burghardt family, who had been free people since the American Revolution.

"I collected all my personal property which I could take with me," William later wrote, "my books; my grandfather's wrought iron tongs and shovel; I kept a few pieces of the blue china which all my life had graced the Thanksgiving and Christmas table. I longed for the great brass kettle in which Grandmother Burghardt had washed and made soap, but I was dissuaded."

The young Du Bois, handsome, delicately built, with dark hair and brown skin, happily entered the unfamiliar world at Fisk. He had been almost a lone black as a student in Great Barrington. But at Fisk he was inspired by the sight of black men and women of all shades—black, brown, yellow, and near-white. He said, "A new loyalty and allegiance replaced my Americanism: henceforward I was a Negro."

Fisk University had been founded at the end of the Civil War by the American Missionary Society as the training-ground for the ablest black youth, who would, in turn, become leaders of their race in America as well as Africa. Like Atlanta University in Georgia and Howard University in Washington, D.C., Fisk was supported by white philanthropy from the North and South, and drew its black students from all over the South. Compared to William Du Bois, the students from Georgia, Alabama, Mississippi, Louisiana, were worldly men and women who had seen the horrors of lynchings and had faced the howl of white mobs.

A black seventeen-year-old from New England was a rarity at Fisk. William began as a sophomore because of his excellent high school training, and his classmates were at least five to ten years older than he. William quickly became a curiosity, even to his teachers. When in October he came down with a severe case of typhoid fever, the whole campus waited anxiously for his recovery.

A few weeks later the annual schoolwide examination took place. The exam gave the poorly trained student a chance to review reading, writing, and arithmetic. William ranked second; the white German teacher's daughter, Mary Bennett, was ahead of him. He couldn't quite forgive Mary for being first, since she was not only a girl, but was white. Furthermore, he knew that the test hadn't been fair for most of the students, who had been poorly trained in the South's impoverished black public schools.

"Nevertheless," William wrote, "my popularity rather went to my head. I was bright, but sharp-tongued and given to joking hard with my fellows.

Some resented this and I remember C. O. Hunter, a big, black, earnest boy near twice my size who resented some quip of mine. He took me so firmly by the arm that I winced. He said, 'Don't you do that again!' I didn't."

CHAPTER 3

HAVING HIS FIRST formal supper at Fisk University, William sat opposite two of the most beautiful young black women he had ever seen. "I promptly lost my appetite," he later wrote, "but I was deliriously happy!" Black women students sat next to him in his classes and he talked to them, sometimes choking with shyness, but more often eagerly pouring forth to them his dreams.

The three years at Fisk were a time of great development for William. He learned about southern prejudice and discrimination firsthand. Everywhere and in every public manner he was forced to exist separately from whites. The insult and abuse he might receive at any time always shocked him. Once, on a street in Nashville, he brushed against a white woman quite by accident. Cordially he raised his hat by way of apology. The bitter sneer and contempt shown by the white woman caused him never to raise his hat again to a southern white. He was at first amazed to discover that many of his fellow students at Fisk carried guns, but he quickly understood that violence was a reality and a constant threat to all the black students.

During William's years at Fisk, lynching of blacks was on the rampage in the South. Between 1885 and 1894, there were 1,700 blacks lynched in the United States. Ida Wells Barnett, the black crusader against lynching, was driven out of Memphis, Tennessee, where as an editor of the *Free Press* she wrote column after outraged column against these criminal acts. In 1892 a black man was burned at the stake. Other blacks were hanged and then shot. In the North and in William's serene New England no one seemed to care.

Frederick Douglass, the former slave, now a national spokesman for his people, wrote in 1892: "Let the press and the pulpit of the South unite their power against the cruelty, disgrace and shame that is settling like a mantle of fire upon these lynch-law States, and lynch-law itself will soon cease to exist."

If the press and the pulpit of the South had the power, they made no effort to wield it. And William Du Bois became truly black as every aspect of black experience, including lynching, became forever imprinted on his mind.

However, as a young student, William had no overwhelming desire to cause any revolutionary change in the way life seemed to be. He decided that in his own time he would work to help better the conditions of his black people. But he thoroughly expected that they would come to better themselves quite naturally, and largely through education. As did most people of his time, William believed that society was an unchanging foundation upon which the present culture was laid. Men might expand and improve the culture, but the foundation of democracy was a permanent base of security.

Today, in the last phase of the twentieth century, the world's people view an age in which the foundations of life and society seem to be tottering. Black militancy, with its demand for true equality at once, is loud and clear. A fair share of the young, as well as the old, are openly critical of war and its high cost in lives and money. Revolutionary students throughout the world are straining against the established order of education, government, and economic systems.

Such a widespread, profound questioning of society and its institutions was unheard of in William Du Bois' young manhood. But the violence committed against black people saved William from ever conforming completely to the attitudes of his time.

As William studied at Fisk, America and Europe were in a period of industrial expansion. Cities were becoming the centers of life. Inventions were marvelous: the telephone, the harnessing of electricity, and the development of the internal combustion engine.

In 1859 Charles Darwin's *Origin of Species* was published. Darwin's biological research contributed to the growing belief among Americans that the spoils of the world belonged to the nations which were strong. In nature, said Darwin, more individuals were born in a species than could live out a normal span of life. There took place a *struggle for existence* between the weakest of the species and those with the characteristics most useful for getting along in the environment. The *fittest* survived by means of *natural selection* because they were always able to adapt themselves to changing conditions. The strains of a species which had the best survival powers were the *most favored races*.

Darwin's theory was meant to be purely biological and was used wrongly in a social context to justify the claim that whites were, and always would be, superior to blacks, and to demonstrate that those who had wealth deserved it. The rich had obviously proved themselves "fitter" than the poor and wretched of the earth! Men such as John Fiske and Reverend Josiah Strong wrote books and gave lectures proclaiming the Anglo-Saxon race destined "by God and evolution" to rule the world. Such racism influenced generations of historians to ignore the important contributions of darker races to the world's civilizations. Europe, America, and Great Britain apologized for seizing nations and their resources by saying that it was the destiny of the strong to conquer the weak. Using this sort of logic, business had an excuse to seize markets for its goods all over the earth; and wealth became God.

"The poor planned to be rich," William Du Bois

wrote years later in his life, "and the rich planned to be richer."

This climate of thinking determined what William and other college students of his time would learn and know. It would have been asking too much of him to have him question this world movement around him. It hadn't occurred to him that what the white world was doing might not be right. He wondered only why his black brothers were refused a part in this seemingly beautiful world.

At Fisk William's relationship with his teachers was fine and exciting. Frederic Chase taught him natural science, and Adam Spence taught him Greek. The president of Fisk, Erastus Cravath, was a man who William felt was completely honest. Such excellence among the teaching staff inspired him to begin building his program for "freedom and progress among Negroes."

About this time, William founded the *Fisk Herald,* the college newspaper. As its editor he wrote "An Open Letter to the Southern People," in which he expressed to the South his hope that educated blacks and whites would unite to lead and help the ignorant and poor. He warned the white South that it faced sheer hatred from blacks if it did not grant them equality soon. The South answered William's letter with silence. Few knew or cared about the scribblings of a college youth who took himself so seriously and was black, besides.

In order to be of service to his people, William was eager to know as much as he possibly could about the way in which they lived day by day—what they worried about and what they dreamed. For this reason he decided to teach during the summers far out in the countryside of Tennessee. East Tennessee, where he wished to go, was no more than fifty miles from Fisk; yet it was a world totally different from the one he knew at college. He entered a Teachers' Institute at the county seat, where prospective teachers were taught spelling, fractions, "and other mysteries—white teachers in the morning, Negroes at night."

Finally William and the others were ready to leave the institute and begin their search for schools:

I learned from hearsay (for my mother was mortally afraid of fire-arms) that the hunting of ducks and bears and men is wonderfully interesting, but I am sure that the man who has never hunted a country school in the South has something to learn of the pleasures of the chase. I see now the white, hot roads lazily rise and wind and fall before me under the burning July sun: I feel the deep weariness of heart and limb as ten, eight, six miles stretch relentlessly ahead; I feel my heart sink heavily as I hear again and again "Got a teacher? Yes." So I walked on and on—horses were too expensive—until I had wandered beyond railways, beyond stage lines, to a land of "varmints" and rattlesnakes, where the coming of a stranger was an event, and men lived and died in the shadow of one blue hill.[1]

Walking a blistering ten miles a day, William finally found a school in a valley near Alexandria. There had been a black school in this valley only once since the Civil War. Here William taught for two successive terms during the summer and earned for himself nearly $60.

William's schoolhouse was a log hut behind a rail fence. There was no longer a door at the entrance, and the windows consisted of chinks between the logs. The desk he used was made of three boards. His chair was borrowed from the landlady, and he had to return it to her each night. He had hoped for desks and chairs for the students like those of his New England past. But he had to use what was available, so he settled for rough plank benches without backs, sometimes without even legs. There were no chalkboards, hardly any books, and his students had to walk great distances.

"On the other hand," William wrote, "I heard the sorrow songs[2] sung with primitive beauty and grandeur. I saw the hard, ugly drudgery of country life and the writhing of landless, ignorant peasants. I saw the race problem at nearly its lowest terms."

Seeing rural poverty in the South for the first time was a heart-rending yet inspiring experience for William. He met extremely poor, starving blacks and grew to know them well. He would one day immortalize the country black people of eastern Tennessee in a volume of essays entitled *The Souls of Black Folk,* published in 1903. And ten years after his teaching experience,

William would return to the valley, drawn to it again the way one is always compelled to revisit the place of one's "birth." He found his favorite student, Josie, dead. His log schoolhouse was gone, but in a new and slightly better one owned by the county there was a school session every year. His students had grown up, life had changed—but it was no better. Thus, leaving the valley for the last time, William would write in *The Souls of Black Folk:*

> My journey was done, and behind me lay hill and dale, and life and Death. How shall man measure Progress there where the dark-faced Josie lies? How many heartfuls of sorrow shall balance a bushel of wheat? How hard a thing is life to the lowly, and yet how human and real! And all this life and love and strife and failure,—is it the twlight of nightfall or the flush of some faint-dawning day?
>
> Thus sadly musing, I rode to Nashville in the Jim Crow car.[3]

Fisk University had been a good school for William; he liked it, but it was small, with limited facilities and equipment. He yearned to have the best education he could get and at the largest and finest place of organized learning. His first college choice had been Harvard, and eventually he intended to go there. At Harvard he would study the science of all sciences, philosophy, which was the study of the processes that govern thought and conduct.

The need for earning a living at college was not something William thought much about. He had no desire for large amounts of money, but he had to live, and the world didn't pay philosophers much of anything. Thinkers and not men of action, philosophers were of little use in a world of action. Frederic Chase at Fisk pointed this out to him, but to no avail.

President Cravath offered William a scholarship to Hartford Theological Seminary. William had taken part in the religious life at Fisk his first year at the school. Still, by his second year, religion, organized and dogmatic, ceased to have much meaning for him. He rejected President Cravath's offer and for the next several years tried to decide what career he would pursue.

In an effort to make itself a national institution, Harvard in the late 1880s began to encourage good students from the South and the West to apply. And seeing advertisements offering scholarships, William applied to Harvard at once. He wrote the institution that he wished to study the sciences and philosophy. His world now was divided into blacks and whites, and he no longer had any great affection for white Harvard. But he still meant to prepare himself for leadership of his people with the best education possible.

Harvard accepted William immediately, provided he repeat his junior and senior years. Although he had received his Bachelor of Arts degree from Fisk, Harvard felt that the black institution was lagging in scholarly requirements. None of this was of much concern to William, for he wanted to attend Harvard because of the opportunity for wide learning it offered him.

For his senior paper at Fisk William wrote about Otto von Bismarck, a German statesman of that time who had "made a nation out of a mass of bickering peoples." This was the kind of action for which American blacks needed to prepare themselves, William felt: "marching forth with strength and determination under trained leadership."

Bismarck had unified Germany into the German Empire. He had not accomplished this feat by any romantic uplift of a people who loved him, as William at first thought. Bismarck had been a Prussian of the landholding class. Democracy, liberalism, socialism, were all distasteful to him. He didn't understand or trust the bulk of the German states beyond his Prussia, and he was not always bound by principles or ideas. Close unions with other countries were necessities to be honored as long as they were convenient, for the enemy of today could become the good friend of tomorrow. Bismarck became skilled at what is known as *Realpolitik,* or the control and use of power to accomplish one's aims. In the realm of *Realpolitik,* it matters little whether an idea is right or wrong. The question is whether an idea is workable through the proper use of power.

William knew nothing of power politics, and the philosophy of *Realpolitik* could not have been more alien to his belief in the rightness, the truth of his cause. During his three years at Fisk he came to know and understand the so-called Negro Problem much more clearly, and he was certain it could be solved by educated blacks like himself. William knew little of the Industrial Revolution, which had used the enslavement of his people as a means to its own development. His education had barely touched on economics or the theories of Karl Marx, the socialist.

Like most other students at Fisk, William looked forward to a professional career after graduation and had no thought of making revolution.

After graduating from Fisk in June 1888 he needed money to supplement the scholarship given to him by Harvard. So he joined as business manager a small group which called itself simply a Glee Club and which was to spend the summer at Lake Minnetonka near Minneapolis. There members of the Glee Club would become waiters in the summer hotel and afterward give concerts to obtain extra money.

The plan was for William to travel with the Glee Club, work with it during the summer, and then toward the end of the season go on ahead to make a series of singing engagements. The summer over, the Glee Club would return to Fisk, and William would go east to Harvard. The only problem with the plan was the fact that William had never worked in a hotel or waited on tables in his life. He became a busboy, and a poor one at that. He never made tips because he was usually so busy watching the antics of guests in the dining room that he neglected his work. He nearly starved until he discovered that black waiters and busboys had to pilfer their food if they ever hoped to eat adequately. William never could bring himself to pilfer, but hunger forced him to share delicious treats others stole.

The business-manager arrangement turned out to be an important experience for him. He was able to gain an impression of midwestern America as he went about finding singing engagements in Minnesota, Wisconsin and Illinois. He spoke to church leaders and literary groups, who, on the whole, were polite to him. Fortunately the Glee Club was able to make about $100 for each member through its singing, with charming, well-educated William acting as the advance man.

When the summer ended, William started east with only $50, which had to last him until his share of the money from the Glee Club reached him at Harvard. On the train he was "hustled" out of $5 by a fellow black man. William had desperately needed every penny of his money, and the experience with the black man, though enlightening, had hurt his pride as well as his pocketbook. Somewhat grimly he continued on toward Harvard and the teachers who would reveal to him the genius of his own mind.

CHAPTER 4

Wᴵᴸᴸᴵᴬᴹ ᴱᴺ-
tered Harvard as a junior in 1888. The university was
236 years old and was considered one of the finest institutions of higher education America had to offer.
But southern white students refused to sit near William
in class, and northern whites tended to ignore him outside of class. He tried joining student organizations
but felt unwelcome. Increasingly he was isolated,
lonely, and believed himself rejected by his fellow students. Some of this sensitivity resulted from his own
New England aloofness and his acid remarks. However,
much of what he felt was actual race prejudice against
him.

At Fisk William had been a member of a closed
racial group; by the time he came to Harvard, the idea
of race separation was quite strong in him. He avoided
contact with white students, in part because he feared
their insults, but also he took for granted that they and
he were training for different careers in worlds that

would be essentially separate. Furthermore, he disliked the fantasy held by whites that blacks desired most of all to associate with them. Unhappily, he gave up courting a black girl who looked white, because he would have resented people thinking he had married outside his race.

William found his friends among the black people of Boston and surrounding places. He escorted the prettiest girls he could find to various gatherings; the *Harvard Crimson,* the campus newspaper, took note of his girl friends. Often he was insulted, such as the time at a reception when a white woman seemed "determined" to mistake him for a waiter.

The fact was that William lived within a completely self-imposed black world, which was self-sufficient but narrow-minded. He ignored as much as he could the closed white world that had made necessary the black one. And although he was never arrogant toward whites, he was not fawning and shuffling, either. He continued to make social contacts along racial lines, even though many of his black friends resented his race loyalty. They were quick to point out to him that he was mulatto, not black; that he was a northerner, not a southerner, and need not concern himself with the problems of poor blacks in the South. His friends felt that race distinctions had to go, and the sooner the better. William agreed with them to some extent. But he soon began to stress cultural differences between blacks and whites which he believed were much too important for blacks to lose in the mixture that was "integrated" America.

More and more he believed in voluntary race segregation, while his black friends continued to hope for a complete and rapid integration of the races on almost any terms. Clearly, the two main streams of Afro-American thought in the twentieth century—black separatism on the one hand and integration on the other—were already the serious concern of black students in the nineteenth century.

William's friends insisted that he and they were completely different from the mass of blacks and shouldn't worry themselves about the poor blacks' condition. In turn, he reasoned that his black friends made racial distinctions which might one day tear the race apart. Some of these friends wouldn't associate with dark-skinned Negroes for fear of being singled out and discriminated against. William despised the high regard they gave to blacks with lighter complexions. However, he understood how the fears of his friends had developed. For across the country, racist newspapers and magazines pounded into black people and all America the myth of the "inborn inferiority" of the black race.

Although William felt alienated from white students because of racial myths and culture, he found his teachers at Harvard to be without prejudice. He was accepted as a young man with an excellent mind by Harvard's leading intellectuals and scholars.

"This cutting off of myself from my white fellows, or

being cut off," William wrote, "did not mean unhappiness or resentment. I was in my early manhood, unusually full of high spirits and humor. I thoroughly enjoyed life. I was conscious of understanding and power, and conceited enough still to imagine, as in high school, that they who did not know me were the losers, not I."

Hoping to make philosophy his career, William studied under philosophers William James and George Santayana. He intended to teach to support himself and took courses in chemistry, geology, social science, and philosophy. William James guided him to pragmatism, a system of philosophy which tests the truth of any idea by its practical results. Albert Bushnell Hart taught William history and the techniques of documentary research. With Frank William Taussig, the political economist, he studied what would later become known as sociology.

The subject of race was discussed in William's classes, and he heard lectures on the evolution of man. He was told that there were obvious differences among the various races. It was evident to him from these lectures that the majority held the opinion that the lowest status belonged to blacks. However, at Harvard, the current theory of social evolution held that black people could advance to the level of white people within a reasonable period of time. William saw no reason at all to doubt this theory.

William joined the Philosophical Club and was a member of an eating club which allowed him to buy his meals more cheaply. From James, Taussig, and another teacher, Ephraim Emerton, he received invitations to dinners and to receptions. However, William continued to know very little about the Harvard of white students. He didn't even know about Phi Beta Kappa, the honorary society of American college students of high scholastic achievement. He knew nothing of important social groups on campus. He was at Harvard for education, and with that education he meant to broaden his idea of the meaning of the universe.

By the time he was twenty-three years old, William realized that the so-called Negro Problem could be examined as "a vast economic mistake" established and supported by the white southern power structure. The "mistake" was the exclusion of black workers from the labor market and the exploitation of white workers, and he knew that political participation would allow all workers to protect their economic interests.

William advanced the theory that the problems of the South might be solved through the organization of a brain trust and the building of a university system. The South had tried to use the grammar and industrial school as an educational foundation, believing strongly that universities for blacks were not needed. He began to see the college-trained black as the advisor of an educated, politically active working class. Among this group of professional men, students, and white-collar workers, he grew aware of a common bond of color. All of them had a similar history of slavery or oppression and a present-day experience of prejudice and discrimination. William foresaw his group as being exactly the same as thousands of other black groups across the country. Their pattern of culture made them a related mass of people, and this we know to be true today. But eighty years ago the idea that a black man in Boston or New York might be closer to a black man in Chicago than to the white man on the next street was something of a revelation.

Having familiarized himself with the black community of Boston, William believed it was time to inform that group of what he thought was wrong with the black race. In a speech before The National Colored League of Boston he denounced politicians and those who did nothing but talk. He criticized the black ministry and its churches for doing so little to improve the lives of their members. Finally, he concluded that blacks, unused to libraries, uninterested in higher education, were in many ways responsible for their own situation.

William's honesty was seen as egotism by the black community which had so graciously accepted him. Never meaning to offend anyone, William had simply been extremely earnest in his desire to inform and inspire his people. It was his obligation, he felt, to express his ideas to blacks as well as whites.

So he lived, carefully expressing his thoughts, however unpopular they might be. He had a sharp tongue.

Always critical, he was not unhappy or resentful. Never well-dressed, he did manage to clothe himself decently. Good manners were never very important to him, and he developed a lofty impatience which often frightened people away.

He wrote, "I was in Harvard, but not of it, and realized all the irony of my singing 'Fair Harvard.' I sang it because I liked the music."

In June 1890 William received his bachelor of arts degree *cum laude* (with praise) in philosophy, and he was one of five students selected to speak at Commencement. As his subject he chose Jefferson Davis, who from 1861 to 1865 was the first and only president of the southern Confederacy. William had pointedly chosen Davis in order to bring to Harvard and the nation a discussion of slavery. He also meant to reveal the kind of civilization that had been represented by the president of the Confederate States of America.

Through Jefferson Davis' life and times, William examined America's hero-worship of the strong man whose "Individualism" was "coupled with the rule of might." The strong man was willing and ready to advance his own civilization by killing American Indians and enslaving Africans.

During the Mexican War Jefferson Davis had commanded the Mississippi Rifles. He had been wounded and was a hero to many people. To William, Davis was a "hero of a national disgrace called by courtesy the Mexican War."[2]

The strong man and his mighty Right Arm has become the Strong Nation with its armies. Under whatever guise, however a Jefferson Davis may appear as man, as race, or as a nation, his life can only logically mean this: the advance of a part of the world at the expense of the whole; the overwhelming sense of the I, and the consequent forgetting of the Thou. . . . A system of human culture whose principle is the rise of one race on the ruins of another is a farce and a lie.

William's Commencement speech created a sensation, and *The Boston Herald* quoted the praise given him by Bishop Henry C. Potter of New York: "When at the last commencement of Harvard University I saw a young colored man appear . . . and heard his brilliant and eloquent address, I said to myself: 'Here is what an historic race can do if they have a clear field, a high purpose, and a resolute will.' "

Since the age of six, William had been in school continuously and had more education than most white or black men twice his age. He understood fully what an important opportunity Harvard had been for him. There he had formed logical work habits with the hours of the day planned to the minute—habits that would remain with him through the rest of his long life. He had studied with fine teachers who were pleased to know him, and he had become a serious student who knew what he wanted. Slowly now, his thinking began to center on the struggle of his people for equality.

By 1890 the South had enacted laws that denied

almost all blacks the right to vote. And until 1910 mainly whites would be able to vote in the southern states. During the same period, most of the segregation laws were passed that applied to schools, churches, graveyards, and other public places. Black people were degraded in magazines, songs, cartoons, newspapers, jokes, and nursery rhymes. They were called "dangerous" as well as "stupid" and "childlike." William was deeply enraged by it all.

Throughout the world this racist reaction to nonwhite peoples continued. France, England, and Germany no longer made excuses for dividing the resources of Africa among themselves in the name of God, Christianity, and the "Advance of Civilization." The Germans took colonies in the Cameroons and Togo on the west coast, established a protectorate called German East Africa, and annexed a desert they called German Southwest Africa. The French took most of western Africa, starting at Algeria and going south across the Sahara Desert and the French Sudan to points on the coast of Guinea. To Britain went Rhodesia, Kenya, and Uganda. Egypt had been a British protectorate since 1812.

This wholesale grabbing of lands affected even the teaching at Harvard, for students like William were taught nothing that might cause them to question the aggression of European powers toward less militant countries. As William wrote, "Here was England with her flag draped around the world, ruling more black folk than white and leading the colored peoples of the earth to Christian baptism, and as we assumed, to civilization and eventual self-rule."

The United States was also moving toward imperialism. The country's industry thought it needed new foreign markets, and many looked to a future when the American people would become leaders of the world.

In 1890 William became a fellow in the Harvard Graduate School and seriously applied William James' pragmatism and Albert Bushnell Hart's research methods to the social sciences. Of significance to his future black world was the fact that he now began research into black history. Mastering the methods of science— of experiment, observation, and study—he applied them to the unheard-of field of black studies.

William fully intended to continue his studies until he had obtained his Ph.D. degree. For his doctoral thesis he chose the suppression of the African slave trade to America. Painstakingly he sifted through the laws of the colonies and the states, United State statutes, and such sources as the Congressional records of that period. Eventually he found more than a hundred important statutes dealing with the slave trade from the middle of the seventeenth century to 1788. His research, in preliminary form, was first published under the title "The Enforcement of the Slave Trade Laws" in the Annual Report of the American Historical Association for 1891.

He was elected to the American Historical Society

and was asked to speak in Washington at the society's meeting in December 1892. The *New York Independent* wrote about his paper:

> The article upon the "Enforcement of the Slave Laws" was written and read by a black man. It was thrilling when one could, for a moment, turn his thoughts from listening to think that scarcely thirty years have elapsed since the war that freed his race, and here was an audience of white men listening to a black man—listening, moreover, to a careful, cool, philosophical history of the laws which had not prevented the enslavement of his race. . . ."[2]

William had searched for "basic knowledge" with which he might in some way guide American blacks, and had come to the study of sociology by way of philosophy and history. He continued to work on his doctoral thesis. Now twenty-four, he had B.A. degrees from Fisk and Harvard, as well as a master's degree from Harvard, and was working toward his Ph.D. degree. With this brilliant start, he made up his mind to study in Europe, preferably in Germany, where the universities were considered the best and where, traditionally, only the best scholars were trained.

William applied to the Slater Fund for a grant or loan of money. The fund had been established for the education of Negroes in 1882; on its board of trustees in 1890 was the former United States president Rutherford B. Hayes. Finally William obtained a grant of

$750, half of which was a loan at 5 percent interest. He didn't mind that part of the grant was in the form of a loan. He was completely happy, and he and his professors agreed that careful training in a European university for at least a year was most important. The Slater Fund had also promised that the grant to William would be renewed for a second year.

"I remember rushing down to New York and talking with ex-President Hayes in the old Astor House, and emerging walking on air. I saw an especially delectable shirt in a shop window. I went in and asked about it. It cost three dollars, which was about four times as much as I had ever paid for a shirt in my life; but I bought it."

CHAPTER 5

WILLIAM'S OP-
portunity to study abroad changed forever his outlook
on life. He was in Germany from 1892 to 1894, removed from the world of America. Being alone and
black in an alien land served not only to reveal William
to himself, but to demonstrate to him that it was possible in the world to have a white culture without color
prejudice. As a black man, he expected discrimination
based on color wherever he went. At Harvard he had
conditioned himself to ignore the cold, hateful stares
of white students who moved away from him when he
sat down to eat or entered a classroom. In Germany
the color of his skin created no barrier whatsoever. He
could go about as a man and need not always remind
himself of the danger his blackness might cause him.

William traveled peacefully in England, France,
Italy, and Germany. He encountered no race prejudice,
but he was aware of the rise of German anti-Semitism
and correctly likened it to the race problem at home in

America. A German family befriended him, and a German girl became infatuated with him. In the student beer halls in Berlin he found that he was as welcome as anyone else. Nowhere did he encounter the brutal barriers that had so walled in his life in America. With a sense of relief, he found it unnecessary to shrink away from people and places in order to protect himself from insult.

The young Du Bois, so very talented, had lived a sheltered and fairly secure life compared to most American blacks. But he had not escaped the emotional turmoil and mental anguish experienced by all blacks, caused by endless race prejudice.

William's background and his experience at Harvard, where professors treated him with respect as an equal, was cause for his believing that the university system and higher education might one day rid the world of race prejudice.

At the University of Berlin his knowledge in the social sciences was broadened by his teachers and by students who came from Russia, Belgium, Poland, Italy, and France. Studying under such historians as Gustav Schmoller and Adolf Wagner, he began to bring together politics, economics, and history. Gustav Schmoller was always warmly friendly to William and had one of the finest reputations in Germany. He influenced William to choose a career dedicated to scholarship. His concern and help did much to convince William that intellectuals were above narrow prejudices.

William was attracted to the socialist movement at the University of Berlin. The Marxist socialist doctrine taught that the authority of the state was a scheme used by the rich, governing class to exploit the masses. The German theorist Karl Marx had been mentioned at Harvard as one whose theories were doubtful. With his collaborator, Friedrich Engels, Marx had developed a system of thought for bringing about a new economic and social order through revolution. In 1848 the *Communist Manifesto* was published, in which Marx and Engels showed how the future revolution would come about.

Throughout history, the Marxists said, class struggle had brought about historical change. The capitalist state contained the "seeds of its own decay" and would eventually be overcome, replaced by a classless, socialist society in which the means of production would be owned by the state and not by a few individuals. At Berlin William was keenly attracted to this doctrine of equality, but he had to conclude that Marxism was too difficult for a student such as himself with little background in its history or development. However, he realized that masses of people over the world were struggling to free themselves from exploitation: " I began to see the race problem in America, the problem of the peoples of Africa and Asia, and the political development of Europe as one."

The Germany of 1892 was a nation of parades and patriotism. German students sang *Deutschland, Deutsch-*

land über Alles, über Alles in der Welt. ("Germany, Germany, over everything, over everything in the world"). Their overwhelming love for their country was the kind of unabashed love William, whose progenitor had been a slave, had difficulty feeling. But enough of German nationalism rubbed off so that he copied some of the manner and appearance of the German kaiser, the king of Prussia. The kaiser always led the parades and pageantry. He rode ahead of his troops on his fine horse through the Brandenburg gate, "With banners gaily flying, with trumpet and with drum!" William trimmed his mustache and beard to the shape of the Kaiser's.

It was the cultural contacts William made in Europe that so greatly changed his life at this time. Music was taken quite seriously in Berlin, and, for the first time, William attended operas and listened to symphonies. He visited the most important art galleries of Europe to see beautiful paintings and great sculpture.

On the occasion of his twenty-fifth birthday William wrote a long entry in his diary, which showed how clearly he saw himself as a historic, ambitious man whose main purpose was to make better the lives of black people:

> . . . The hot dark blood of a black forefather is beating at my heart, and I know that I am either a genius or a fool . . . I am firmly convinced that my own best development is not one and the same with the best

development of the world and here I am willing to sacrifice. That sacrifice to the world's good becomes too soon sickly sentimentality. I therefore take the world that the Unknown lay in my hands and work for the rise of the Negro people, taking for granted that their best development means the best development of the world . . . .

"These are my plans: to make a name in science, to make a name in literature and thus to raise my race. Or perhaps to raise a visible empire in Africa through England, France or Germany. I wonder what will be the outcome? Who knows?[1]

After two years of study at the University of Berlin, at the age of twenty-six, William knew he had received an unusual education for an American of any color. Now he would come home to find a job, to begin his work, and he looked forward eagerly to the prospect.

But the winter of 1893–94 had revealed mounting economic troubles in the United States. Fear gripped Americans as eight thousand businesses failed between April and October 1893. Banks folded, railroads went bankrupt, and unemployment in the cities reached the extraordinary level of 4.5 million. Not only were the workers of the cities hard hit, but the United States government was forced to seek a loan of $65 million in gold from the financial syndicate of J. Pierpont Morgan. Discontent spread through the rural Midwest as, in the summer of 1894, searing heat and winds reduced the corn crop by three fourths from the previous year. As more city workers lost their jobs or went on half pay, bands of unemployed men roamed the country, finally to begin the first march on Washington.

No one cared about what was happening to black people at this time, including the Congress of the United States, which had in 1894 repealed the so-called Force Acts. These acts had given the president the power to move against secret organizations such as the Ku Klux Klan and the Knights of the White Camellia, whose business was maiming and murdering blacks to keep them from voting. Now the federal government refused to try any longer to protect the voting rights of black people.

To these serious problems of America William Du Bois returned. His immediate concern was to earn a living: "I was not exacting or hard to please. I just got down on my knees and begged for work, anything and anywhere."

Finally, he received three offers of work. The first came from Wilberforce University in southwestern Ohio, at a salary of $800 a year, which he accepted at once. The second offer had come from Lincoln Institute in Missouri, and the last from Booker T. Washington at Tuskegee Institute in Alabama.

He went to Wilberforce in August 1894 and stayed there for two years. The weather was oppressive when William arrived, but he must have made a cool and striking appearance. He wore the Van Dyke beard copied after the German kaiser's. He was lean, and thus seemed taller than his medium height. He was able to hide, somewhat, his receding hairline by wearing a silk hat. He wore gloves and carried a cane, as did most German students he had known.

Said to be a "learned professor just from Germany," William was hired to teach Latin and Greek at Wilberforce, but soon found himself teaching English and German as well. He helped in the discipline of students and would have liked to teach sociology, but this the administration of the school would not permit.

Wilberforce University had been founded by the black bishop Daniel Payne, who had purchased the school from white Methodists. It was administered by the African Methodist Episcopal Church and received funds from the state of Ohio, an arrangement which tended to complicate its administration and caused all manner of friction between church and state.

From the very first William was in difficulty at the school. His manner was too blunt, and, as he said himself, he had "rather inflated ideas" as to what a university ought to be. Wilberforce required attendance at church services and forbade any association between men and women on campus. William once wandered into a prayer meeting only to have the student in charge announce that "Professor Du Bois will lead us in prayer." William answered, "No, he won't!" and nearly lost his job.

The university was the largest school run by the A.M.E. Church. And its influence in the black community was so widespread that as an institution it came to be almost political first and religious second. It was the center of black social life and at the same time was seriously religious. There were church revivals on campus which lasted for a week at a time. William was so thoroughly annoyed by such religious fervor in the midst of serious academic thought that he locked himself in his room for as long as a revival might last.

Sunday school was also an unhappy task for William. The Bible was taken as truth, word for word, and his intelligence demanded that the written word, like everything else, be subject to hard, scientific appraisal. Any interpretation of the Scriptures, however, was forbidden by college policy.

William had to admit to being self-centered and self-satisfied at that time. But perhaps he had a certain right to be, for he had accomplished much in his twenty-six years. "My redeeming feature," he wrote, "was infinite capacity for work and terrible earnestness, with appalling and tactless frankness."

Each day he instructed his students in Latin, Greek, German, and English. He took part in the social life of the school, also, and began to write books. His second published work was his Harvard doctoral thesis, expanded from the preliminary study published in 1891. Entitled *The Suppression of the African Slave Trade, 1638–1870,* it was the first book published in the Harvard Historical Series of 1896. Moreover, it was William's first major scholarly presentation and an attempt to survey the failure to enforce laws against the slave trade. As such, the book was an exhaustive study, so much so that he came to believe that its very thoroughness set it apart from the "total flow of history."[2] Eventually he saw that the book was relatively a small part of the mass of history of which he knew little, and thus it lacked relationship to the whole.

Whatever its limitations, the volume was a tremendous feat for a young scholar. Later it would land him a job at the University of Pennsylvania. The book received favorable reviews. Today the work still stands as an excellent historical study.

Now William was a Doctor of Philosophy, having received his Ph.D. the same year his thesis was published. At the age of twenty-eight, after two years at Wilberforce, he felt unable to take any longer the religious tone of the school, where a good education was thought to include religious ceremonies and revivals. The battles between the politicians of state and church constantly infuriated him. And he found that his plan to free his race through history and social science by means of research and writing would never proceed at Wilberforce as long as he was forced to teach in established fields.

That very year of 1896 he was offered a fifteen-month appointment at the University of Pennsylvania, which he happily accepted. Dr. Charles C. Harrison, the provost of the University, was aware of his fine work in the field of black history. He granted him a special fellowship to conduct a study of the black community in Philadelphia's Seventh Ward slums. The young Dr. Du Bois was given the rank of Assistant Instructor in Sociology, although he didn't teach, at a salary of $900 a year. At this time he married Nina Gomer, the daughter of a chef in a hotel in Cedar Rapids, Iowa. He had met Nina at Wilberforce. Her mother, who had died, had been born in Alsace, which was then part of Germany.

The Doctor and his young wife came to live in Philadelphia after three months of marriage. They settled down in one room over a cafeteria in the slums of the Seventh Ward. There Dr. Du Bois began studying the black people of the district. He had long believed that the world accepted myths about black people because it had no idea what the truth was. For example, white Philadelphians never thought of blacks as individuals, but only as a group. These whites saw racial mixing and intermarriage as the awful results of letting blacks have equality. Such unrealistic fear of integration they used as an excuse for putting a stop to any advancement the blacks might make. Through scientific investigation, William Du Bois was certain he could collect a body of knowledge about his race that would put an end to such ignorance.

The block-by-block survey he made in the Seventh Ward showed his vast creative energy and his exceptional patience. "I started with no 'research methods,' " he wrote in his autobiography. ". . . I asked little advice as to procedure. The problem lay before me. Study it. I studied it personally . . . I sent out no canvassers. I went myself."

He talked with some five thousand people in all, mapped the whole of the district, and classified it by conditions. Working day and night and with remarkable swiftness, he gathered the history of the black Philadelphian for two centuries.

He had completed his study by the spring of 1898, and it was published a year later. Entitled *The Philadelphia Negro,* it was a labor of love as well as a work of science. Furthermore, it laid the groundwork, Du Bois felt, for solving the problems of black people living in large urban areas. Nearly fifty years later, in 1944, the Swedish sociologist Gunnar Myrdal called *The Philadelphia Negro* a classic study of black community life.

Solid though it was, *The Philadelphia Negro* was never widely read in its own time or later. It was out of print for almost half a century and was only reissued in 1967.

Reviewers in 1899 were quick to praise Dr. Du Bois' cool objectivity and well-reasoned conclusions based on evidence. And well they should have been, for his study had been made in one of the most discouraging of times for black people since the Civil War. It was the period when whites never questioned the belief that fixed laws of superiority and inferiority forever divided the races from one another. The white Anglo-Saxons were thought to be forever superior; they stood at the summit of the mountain of destiny. All other races clamored frantically below, with the blacks prostrate at the very bottom.

William Du Bois' carefully documented evidence in *The Philadelphia Negro* revealed the startling fact that beyond the home environment "there is a far mightier influence to mold and make the citizen, and that is the social atmosphere which surrounds him; first, his daily companionship, the thoughts and whims of his class; then his recreations and amusements; finally the surrounding world of American civilization."[3]

Whites were unused to thinking that their own attitudes toward blacks might affect the way blacks reacted to them or acted toward one another. People in general, black as well as white, tended to see black people as one single mass whose members were exactly the same. But the Doctor's study showed for the first time that American blacks could be divided into classes with assorted life styles and aims. There were the middle classes, the working people, fairly poor to comfortable, the poor, and the vicious and criminal classes.

The idea that classes existed among black people was unheard of, for blacks were usually judged by the criminals among them. It was this class that reinforced easily the time's familiar stereotype of the Negro as stupid but dangerous.

"Thus," wrote Dr. Du Bois, "the class of Negroes which the prejudices of the city [of Philadelphia] have distinctly encouraged is that of the criminal, the lazy and the shiftless; for them the city teems with institutions and charities; . . . for them Philadelphians are thinking and planning; but for the educated and industrious young colored man who wants work and not platitudes, wages and not alms, just rewards and not sermons—for such colored men Philadelphia apparently has no use."[4]

William Du Bois believed that the most advanced class of any group was an example of the possibilities of the whole group. Although small, a class such as this was a part of the Seventh Ward when he began his study. We know it as the beginning of the black middle class. But in Philadelphia in 1898, the black middle class had been forgotten in any discussion of the Negro. Its members were completely cut off from the middle class of whites. Segregated with all other blacks, it should have taken the leadership of the blacks in the Seventh Ward slums, but the black middle class seemed not to want this role, and the people of the ward were not used to looking to it for leadership.

Dr. Du Bois learned from his study in Philadelphia that being born black didn't mean a man such as himself would have complete knowledge of his own race. He found that he had learned more from the blacks in Philadelphia than he was able to teach them about the problems they faced. But he knew with certainty what his life work would be. For his black people were a living, striving group with a long historical past. And for them he would work toward a theory of sociology;

with accurate research he could prepare the way for future social reform among his people. Moreover, a storehouse of knowledge based on scientific research might lead the government to form a positive national policy toward black people.

In the field of black studies Dr. Du Bois was the first sociologist to use experiment and observation as the basis of his research. He tried in 1899 to interest Harvard, Columbia, and the University of Pennsylvania in a program of scientific study of the black race, but he soon discovered that these universities were not interested. Where, he wondered, would he find the support he needed for his ambitious program? No answer seemed to be forthcoming from the scholarly world. And for the next twenty-five years none of the so-called leading American colleges would give any of their concern to a program for the study of black Americans.

CHAPTER 6

DR. DU BOIS' PRO-
gram for a scientific study of his race was finally
undertaken by Atlanta University, the black institution
situated in Georgia. President Horace Bumstead of
Atlanta asked him to take charge of the university's
work in sociology, an invitation which he happily accepted. In 1897 he became professor of economics and
history at Atlanta, teaching juniors and seniors sociology and history, economics, political science, and
statistics.

Dr. Du Bois rarely left the campus. The local primary
elections were closed to blacks, so he did not vote. He
never went to parks or museums, for he would have
had to sit in sections put aside for blacks or to attend
at separate hours from whites. Visitors wishing to see
him had to seek him out in his book-lined study at the
university. There he was relaxed, touching freely on
the wide range of his ideas.

Dr. Du Bois based his assumption of continued black

progress in America on the education of the so-called Talented Tenth of his people. By this he meant that given the free opportunity, the most able tenth of all blacks would go on to college. After obtaining broader knowledge through higher education, the Talented Tenth would have a duty to guide and to lead the rest of the race toward a fulfilling life. He knew that without black leadership the black American would have to accept white leadership. This had been one of the important insights gained from his Philadelphia Negro study. However, the Talented Tenth concept was often misunderstood by many to mean the education of a black elite. But Dr. Du Bois always insisted that the Talented Tenth was to be the servant of the remaining 90 percent of black people.

At Atlanta he tried to isolate himself in what he termed "the ivory tower of race," but more and more he found that he could not stand outside the problems of America. By 1890 Mississippi had levied a tax on anyone wishing to vote, and this poll tax severely limited the participation of blacks in elections. At the same time Mississippi instituted an "understanding the Constitution" provision as a prerequisite for voting. Having no education, many blacks couldn't read, and asking them to understand and answer questions about the lengthy and often obscure Constitution of the United States was all but impossible. No one asked poorly educated whites these questions. When the U.S. Supreme Court raised no objection to the laws, other southern states copied Mississippi.

As Dr. Du Bois quickly realized, by far the most detrimental blow to civil rights was the 1896 Supreme Court decision in the Plessy *v.* Ferguson case. The question was whether an Alabama law providing for separate railway carriages for the white and "colored" races was constitutional. The law provided that so long as the accommodations were equal, the enforced separation of two races could in no way make one race appear to be inferior to the other. This "separate but equal" doctrine made segregation constitutional.

More important than ever, Dr. Du Bois felt, was the scientific study of his people, the need to gather factual knowledge of their past and present. Enthusiastically he accepted President Bumstead's offer that he take charge of Atlanta University's newly started conferences on the city problems of blacks. The Tuskegee Institute in Alabama and Hampton Institute in Virginia had already initiated a series of conferences in the areas of agriculture and industry. So it was that in 1897 the Doctor began what he called his "real life work."

The conferences at Atlanta University developed into a source of general information about, and a base for wide study of, many aspects of black life—health and welfare, business, higher education, labor, the church, and crime. One of these areas was to be studied and the findings published each year for ten years. After the ten-year cycle had been repeated ten times, the one hundred years of research material about black life would be a source for scholars, educators, and leaders of government.

Each year the *Publications* of Atlanta University included the resolutions of the conferences headed by Dr. Du Bois. But the main body of each published volume was the record and summary of the year's investigation. Attending these yearly meetings were authorities interested in the problems of the South. Booker T. Washington of Tuskegee, the anthropologist Franz Boas, the social reformer Jane Addams, who had founded the Hull House settlement in Chicago in 1889, were a few of many who took part.

The Atlanta *Publications* showed how Dr. Du Bois had surveyed black society, counted his cases, and listed what he saw. Instituting door-to-door inquiries in different cities, he used the questionnaire and interview to obtain information. Thus he was the only sociologist working in the South collecting facts to test his theories. Furthermore, unlike most such studies, the *Publications* presented information in a straightforward manner that the general reader could understand.

After one revealing study Dr. Du Bois concluded that there were not enough people in business who were black. He also asked black consumers to buy from black-owned businesses whenever possible.

In view of the ideas about blacks held at the time by most whites, the results of the Atlanta studies brought to light impressive truths. In one study of morals and manners, for example, Dr. Du Bois disproved the generalization that blacks were lynched because of evidence against them of rape or attempted rape. Investigating a series of lynchings and using the research gathered by others, he had found that less than a fourth of the lynched blacks had been charged with rape. Blacks were lynched simply because whites desperately feared and hated them.

Dr. Du Bois also turned his attention to the continually high black crime rate, a source for smug contempt among southern whites. He found that by depriving blacks of voting rights, of just laws and just courts, of decent jobs and wages, of equal education—in short, of *manhood* and first-class citizenship—the whites had successfully checked black progress at every turn. He concluded that where there could be no self-respect, there would be no reason for ambition. Without these, blacks committed crimes out of desperation.

The Doctor prepared an exhibit for the World's Fair of 1900, held in Paris. By putting his findings on the black American and his problems into plans, charts, and figures, he was able to show what his studies at Atlanta were trying to accomplish. The exhibit won a grand prize and a gold medal.

Naturally, the Doctor was proud of his award. Surely, he thought, the Atlanta conferences would now grow and develop with abundant financial support. But this was not to be the case. Each year the conferences failed to attract funds. And within ten years these black studies would be abandoned because $5,000 a year could not be found to continue them.

When money proved hard to get, Dr. Du Bois began

to wonder where he had failed. Soon he understood that in order for his studies to become successful enough to attract supporters with large amounts of money, he, or someone, would have to bring them to the attention of a much larger public. Unfortunately there wasn't the money to do that either.

Assuming that the world wanted to know the truth about blacks, the Doctor had been certain that once aware of the facts, the world would support the truth. Because all of his own actions were based on reason, he wrongly assumed that the actions of the world were also based on reason. But he was a black man studying blacks, and whites with money surely asked themselves what black people could have to do with the progress of the world.

By 1906 Dr. Du Bois knew his Atlanta studies would end: "I was scarred and a bit grim, but hugging to my soul the divine gift of laughter and withal determined, even into stubbornness, to fight the good fight."

Now he had become violently outspoken against the injustices heaped on black people. He was particularly outraged by the sickening lynchings of blacks by white mobs. These took place nearly five times a week in Georgia. Federal and state laws were openly violated throughout the South, whenever they were in any way liberal. Southern hatemongers such as Ben Tillman and J. K. Vardaman attacked and insulted blacks anytime they had the chance. Mr. Tillman, governor of South Carolina, spoke these words in 1907:

Look at our environment in the South, surrounded, and in a very large number of counties and in two states outnumbered, by the negroes—engulfed, as it were, in a black flood of semi-barbarians. . . . Taught that they are oppressed, and with breasts pulsating with hatred of the whites, the younger generation of negro men are roaming over the land, passing back and forth without hindrance, and with no possibility of adequate police protection to the communities in which they are residing. . . .[1]

Tillman's outrageous remarks make no mention of the bands of roving whites who terrorized and often murdered blacks. At this time, when Dr. Du Bois' Atlanta studies were a scientific success but a financial burden, the horror of lynchings changed his vision forever:

I remember when it first, as it were, startled me to my feet: a poor Negro in central Georgia, Sam Hose, had killed his landlord's wife. I wrote out a careful and reasoned statement concerning the evident facts and started down to the Atlanta *Constitution* office, carrying in my pocket a letter of introduction to Joel Chandler Harris. I did not get there. On the way news met me: Sam Hose had been lynched, and they said that his knuckles were on exhibition at a grocery store farther down on Mitchell Street, along which I was walking. I turned back to the university. I began to turn aside from my work. I did not meet Joel Chandler Harris nor the editor of the *Constitution*.[2]

With lynchings occurring nearly every day, Dr. Du Bois couldn't for long remain the rational scientist. Furthermore, there was no public demand for the significant work he was now doing. The Atlanta *Publications* totaled 2,172 pages and made available to the public, for the first time, an encyclopedia concerning the social conditions of American blacks. And black colleges of the South were graduating black men and women who demanded their rights as citizens but who, nevertheless, were treated by the South as no better than slaves. The presence of educated black youth in the repressive South created an explosive situation. These students had been taught by whites descended from the northern teachers who had come South during Reconstruction to educate the former slaves. And to these white educators now turned the southern white leadership, who wished to avoid race war but who wished as well to stop further black progress.

With this in mind, the Southern Education Board was formed. Composed of educators and industrialists, the Board offered aid to black institutions which focused on industrial education. Soon expanded into the General Education Board, the group adapted a philosophy implying that blacks must be taught to accept what whites were willing to give them. The place of the black man would be that of the silent laborer in a world controlled by whites. University academic training for blacks would have to be discouraged, since whatever they did in the future would depend upon their white employers. The board was frankly hostile toward Atlanta University, because the University wouldn't conform to southern social conventions. At Atlanta both the black students and white faculty used the same dining halls and dormitories. White students were welcome to join the campus community. The General Education Board, as well as the Georgia legislature, withheld funds from Atlanta for these reasons and, as Dr. Du Bois suspected, because he was associated with the school.

Advised by Booker T. Washington, founder and president of the famous industrial school for blacks, Tuskegee Institute, the General Education Board gave aid to black schools for special training programs in farming in order for them to develop a contented black labor force. In line with Mr. Washington's opinion— since blacks were unskilled and ignorant, they should begin at the bottom level of toil—blacks would be limited to farm work, unskilled labor in industry, and domestic service. The well-paid skilled jobs in labor and management would go to whites. Never was there a more brutal planned economic arrangement, other than slavery itself.

As diabolical as it may sound, this kind of program of oppressing and discriminating against black people was developed and carried out until after World War I. Bearing testimony to the success of the plan were the disenfranchisement laws passed between 1890 and

1910 by all the former slave states and declared constitutional by the United States courts.

This "racial philosophy" of black economic slavery needed a black man who could give it status and common appeal. The president of Tuskegee, Booker T. Washington, had long believed that black progress would come only when and if whites would allow it. He fully intended to get along with the white South in a humble, yet honest and neighborly, fashion. Thus he came to be viewed by the whites as the perfect leader for black people.

As Dr. Du Bois' Atlanta *Publications* were coming to an end, the white South contributed greatly toward making Booker T. Washington the recognized leader of all blacks in America. No discussion of Dr. William Du Bois can proceed without regard for the thinking and actions of this shrewd, highly intelligent gentleman.

CHAPTER 7

B OOKER TALIA-
FERRO Washington was the son of a plantation cook
and a white man he would never know. On April 5,
1856, he was born a slave belonging to James Bur-
roughs of Franklin County, Virginia, and he was freed
by the Emancipation Proclamation of 1863. At fifteen
he toiled long hours each day in a West Virginia salt
mine; at night he taught himself to read. He worked his
way as a janitor through Hampton Institute on the
Virginia coast. Hampton was one of a group of schools
established for blacks after the Civil War, where students could work and study at the same time.

By the time he was twenty, Booker T. Washington
was on the staff of Hampton as a teacher. Next he was
offered the job of principal of the Normal School for
Colored Teachers at Tuskegee, Alabama. The state
legislature of Alabama would pay the teachers' sal-
aries, but no actual school existed. There were no
buildings, no land, no desks, no books, and no students.

Nevertheless, he accepted the position and went on to build from nothing Tuskegee Institute, the most powerful black school America had ever known. Eventually Booker T. Washington became so respected, he freely spoke and dined with presidents and kings. But, sadly, he could never vote in any election in the state of Alabama because he was black.

At Tuskegee Institute Mr. Washington taught his students the importance of learning a trade and of hard work, and the necessity for depending upon themselves. The students obviously learned their lessons well, for they built most of the college buildings.

Like many other black men, Mr. Washington had become deeply disturbed by the ever-growing racial prejudice in the South. A quarter of a century after the Civil War black people had few representatives in Congress. Local southern governments were solidly in the hands of white segregationists. Mr. Washington feared that if he did not cooperate with these whites, his beloved school, Tuskegee, might be closed. He therefore was forced to learn quickly how to deal with the whites, to convince them that his students wanted only to learn skills to become good carpenters, farmers, and shoemakers. Mr. Washingon's ability to get along with these whites and his enormous achievement in building Tuskegee did much to make him a renowned public figure. Whites soon accepted him as a leader who would make no demands for equality.

In 1895 Mr. Washington had been asked to be one

of the speakers at the great Atlanta Cotton Exposition, where southern business eagerly courted the industrial wealth of the north. The southerners hoped that his presence would show the world that the South had solved its so-called Negro problem. For Mr. Washington, the invitation by powerful, white southern business was an honor. It was also for him a grave responsibility. Everywhere his people were being denied their rights. Ignorant and poor whites violently hated blacks, fearing that the blacks might take their jobs from them. The rich wanted to use blacks only as servants and to employ them as cheaply as possible. Black people could not travel without being segregated. They could not go out in public without risking their safety. What could he say, Mr. Washington wondered, that would give his people hope and, at the same time, not cause the whites to impose further restrictions?

The speech Booker T. Washington presented at the exposition in Atlanta came to be known as the "Atlanta Compromise." He said what he sincerely believed to be true:

As we have proved our loyalty to you in the past, in nursing your children, watching by the sick beds of your mothers and fathers, and often following them with tear-dimmed eyes to their graves, so in the future in our humble way, we shall stand by you with a devotion that no foreigner can approach, ready to lay down our lives, if need be, in defense of yours, interlacing our industrial, commercial, civil, and religious life with yours in a way that shall make the interest of both races one. In all things that are purely social we can be as separate as the fingers, yet one as the hand in all things essential to mutual progress.

. . . The wisest among my race understand that the agitation of questions of social equality is the extremest folly, and that progress in the enjoyment of all the privileges that will come to us must be the result of severe and constant struggle, rather than of artificial forcing. No race that has anything to contribute to the markets of the world is long in any degree ostracized. It is important and right that all privileges of the law be ours, but it is vastly more important that we be prepared for the exercise of these privileges. The opportunity to earn a dollar in a factory just now is worth infinitely more than the opportunity to spend a dollar in an opera house.[1]

The Atlanta Compromise caught the attention of the whole of America. A letter of praise soon came from President Grover Cleveland. The white South praised the speech, but many black leaders such as John Hope, a teacher at Roger Williams University and later president of the Atlanta Baptist College, criticized it severely. John Hope wrote in 1896:

If we are not striving for equality, in heaven's name for what are we living? I regard it as cowardly and dishonest for any of our colored men to tell white people or colored people that we are not struggling for equality. If money, education and honesty will not bring to me as much privilege, as much equality as they bring to

any American citizen, then they are to me a curse, and
not a blessing. . . . Let us not fool ourselves nor be fooled
by others. If we cannot do what other freemen do, then
we are not free. Yes, my friends, I want equality.
Nothing less. I want all that my God-given powers will
enable me to get, then why not equality?[2]

The Atlanta Compromise speech had shocked and
infuriated Dr. Du Bois. At a time when black people
were completely segregated, he felt that Mr. Washington had introduced in the name of all black Americans
a program to appease the whites. The "enjoyment of all
the privileges" of the law alluded to in Mr. Washington's speech, Dr. Du Bois felt, should be open to
blacks. He believed that his people should have the
right to vote, to enjoy social equality, and to educate
their youth according to their ability. Dr. Du Bois
wouldn't hear of waiting a moment longer for the exercise of these rights, for he knew no man could obtain
his rights by throwing them away. Blacks, he said,
were being denied the right to vote at the very moment
Mr. Washington would have them concentrate their
energies on industrial education and making money.
Blacks were being designated inferior by state law;
they were being terrorized, murdered, by local secret
organizations. And higher education was being taken
from them by the withdrawal of financial aid to their
institutions of higher learning.

For Dr. Du Bois black progress meant equal rights
at once and the education of the most talented of

black people, while Booker T. Washington believed that blacks must first become good workers in order to obtain wealth and capital. Mr. Washington felt that Dr. Du Bois' demands for social justice were foolish, for he was certain that equality was a *privilege* his race must *earn*. As he said in his speech, the dollar earned in the factory was far more important to the mass of blacks than the dollar spent in an opera house.

Once economically secure, contended Mr. Washington, blacks could then educate their children as they wished. Therefore he stressed training in skilled and semiskilled trades, and in industry, and instruction in common labor. Above all, he felt that blacks must live humbly and in harmony with their white neighbors.

It becomes clear that the Talented Tenth concept of Dr. Du Bois and the trade-school training ground advocated by Mr. Washington both could have been used to fulfill the needs of black people. Those blacks with ability who wished higher education should have been free to pursue it. Those wishing vocational training should have been trained. American democracy by definition is committed to free and equal education of all its people. The differences between William Du Bois and Booker T. Washington need not have existed, *except* that white America obviously didn't want educated blacks or even skilled ones. What Mr. Washington failed utterly to realize was that his people were being denied both the factory *and* the opera house. This Dr. Du Bois understood clearly. The two men lived with the same deplorable conditions of the deep South but had come to quite opposite conclusions about how to survive them.

Clearly, the obstacle for both men and their programs was the reactionary white South. The conduct of the General Education Board reflected the fact that southerners didn't want academically trained blacks who would learn to argue and question powerful white control of their lives. Nor did they wish to give skilled industrial jobs to blacks at the expense of skilled white workers. Mr. Washington's industrial school, Tuskegee Institute, showed poor results because its graduates always received less money from southern employers than their labor was worth. As long as the employers cheated black workers, the blacks couldn't possibly gain the wealth and capital Mr. Washington wished for them.

The white South wanted solely a subservient black labor force whom it could pay cheaply and manipulate as it pleased. In this respect it was not far removed from the European imperialists who exploited workers in far-off African and Asian colonies; nor from the United States government, which had already annexed Puerto Rico, the Philippine Islands, and the Hawaiian Republic and also exploited workers of these countries.

It was Booker T. Washington's belief that no matter how much blacks might resent current public opinion in the South—that in all things, blacks were inferior to whites—they must go along with it in order to gain more jobs and more wealth. Rich and powerful white men such as Andrew Carnegie praised the Washington point of view and poured money into his Tuskegee Institute.

On the other hand, Dr. Du Bois was convinced that southern public opinion could be forced to change through strong black leadership. It had been the convictions of bigoted southerners that had brought about a rampage of lynchings and all of the Jim Crow legislation. With black strength and leadership. Dr. Du Bois said, these conditions might well be reversed.

His own method of leadership grew out of his formidable ability to persuade through his writing, teaching, and public lectures. At all times he insisted that whites were strangling black institutions of higher education, such as Atlanta University, and denying his people the right to vote. He demanded that Congress force the South to obey the United States Constitution.

Meanwhile, there developed around Mr. Washington at Tuskegee a smooth, well-financed, and very powerful organization which Dr. Du Bois called the Tuskegee Machine. Whites rushed forward with financial aid for projects of the black leader who expressed so well the need for humility and hard work for a subordinate race. During the presidential terms of Theodore Roosevelt and William Howard Taft—from 1901 to 1912—Booker T. Washington became the dispenser of all federal appointments dealing with black Americans. And well did he understand the power the whites so willingly gave him. He used that power to influence the direction black education would take. Brilliant at organization and the manipulation of power, he was regarded by most whites as the leader of all the ten million black people in America. Mr. Washington was said to be one of the most gifted men of his time, and industrialists such as John D. Rockefeller listened to him and valued his advice. The philanthropist Andrew Carnegie made a gift of $600,000 to Tuskegee Institute, while Dr. Du Bois' Atlanta studies were coming to an end because of lack of funds.

No matter how powerful Mr. Washington had become in the minds of whites, his leadership never ceased to be questioned by important blacks. William Monroe Trotter, the fiery black editor of the Boston *Guardian,* believed him to be no better than a traitor to his race. Monroe Trotter had been a brilliant student at Harvard and had received his A.B. degree *magna cum laude* (with great praise) just before Mr. Washington made his Atlanta Compromise speech. He was young, handsome, well-educated, and a leading member of black society in Boston. Yet he had begun to understand that his education and his position meant nothing if the less fortunate members of his race were not free. Mr. Trotter saw blatant southern bigotry relentlessly spreading north as Mr. Washington continued to appease the South.

W. E. B. Du Bois met Trotter when he came to lecture at the Boston Literary and Historical Association, a militant forum which Mr. Trotter had helped to organize. Later, in 1901, Mr. Trotter and two associates, William H. Scott and George W. Forbes, had started the radical newspaper the *Guardian,* which was for and about black Americans. It protested all manner of prejudice and discrimination; and editorial after editorial attacked Mr. Washington's policy of placating the white South.

In July 1903 Mr. Washington was invited to speak by the National Negro Business League of Boston. The meeting was to take place at the African Methodist Episcopal Zion Church. The *Guardian* editors, Monroe Trotter and George Forbes, planned to make Mr. Washington answer in public questions regarding his attitudes on voting and education. On the night of the meeting a disturbance erupted which was magnified by the press into what became known as the Boston Riot. One man was stabbed, and Monroe Trotter was arrested. Dr. Du Bois was horrified to think that anyone would suspect Monroe Trotter of deliberately trying to keep Mr. Washington from being heard; he was furious that his brilliant friend should be put in jail.

No other single incident at this time disturbed the Doctor so much. Deeply angered when Monroe Trotter was found guilty and sentenced to thirty days in jail, he was also discouraged far beyond the matter of the Boston Riot. For an unshakable fact had troubled him for some time. No matter how important his Atlanta studies had been in the scientific evaluation of black progress, he saw that the black American was not making any lasting improvement in his daily life. When blacks *were* able to obtain decent jobs—by working for less money than whites—they were hated and violently attacked by white workers. Black public schools were deteriorating, and there was widespread, woeful poverty among the masses of black people.

Dr. Du Bois' Atlanta studies had gained prestige for him and had given black people some measure of pride in their historical accomplishments. But because of the sometimes faulty research methods used, the studies had not lived up to the Doctor's own view of pure science. The Atlanta *Publications* had, furthermore, drawn criticism from some white scholars who were not accustomed to looking to black leaders on black problems. And, as always, Dr. Du Bois' influence and his considerable achievement were overshadowed by the fame and power of Booker T. Washington.

Mr. Washington's autobiography, *Up from Slavery,* had been published in 1901. He had written other books, but none had done for him as much as did this single volume. *Up from Slavery* was a black success story and was appealing to millions of Americans, both black and white. In its modest approach, the volume told whites of the North and South that they need not worry about blacks attempting to gain immediate equality:

My own belief is, although I have never before said so in so many words, that the time will come when the Negro in the South will be accorded all the political

rights which his ability, character and material posses-
sions entitle him to. I think, though, that the opportunity to freely exercise such political rights will not
come in any large degree through outside or artificial
forcing, but will be accorded to the Negro by the
southern white people themselves, and that they will
protect him in the exercise of these rights. Just as soon
as the South gets over the old feeling that it is
being forced by "foreigners," or "aliens," to do something which it does not want to do, I believe that the
change in the direction that I have indicated is going
to begin. In fact, there are indications that it is already
beginning in a slight degree.[3]

How hopelessly wrong Mr. Washington was. During
the period of the Tuskegee Machine there was little
improvement in race relations in America. The number
of blacks lynched continued to increase each year.

Dr. Du Bois published his answer to this philosophy,
The Souls of Black Folk, in 1903. It was the most successful of his books and the most widely read, and it
became the banner around which rallied all the young
black intellectuals who could not accept the Washington compromise. The book, a collection of essays, expressed the Doctor's personal attitudes and beliefs
concerning black life and criticized the philosophy of
appeasement. It was a lovely and sometimes lonely
statement on being black in America, and it created
a strong link between blacks across the country, who
had for so long a time kept their own feelings of isolation and anguish to themselves. Now these blacks had

found their voice in the subtle, dynamic pen of Dr. Du Bois:

> After the Egyptian and Indian, the Greek and Roman, the Teuton and Mongolian, the Negro is a sort of seventh son, born with a veil, and gifted with second-sight in this American world,—a world which yields him no true self-consciousness, but only lets him see himself through the revelation of the other world. It is a peculiar sensation, this double-consciousness, this sense of always looking at one's self through the eyes of others, of measuring one's soul by the tape of a world that looks on in amused contempt and pity. One ever feels his twoness,—an American, a Negro; two souls, two thoughts, two unreconciled strivings; two warring ideals in one dark body, whose dogged strength alone keeps it from being torn asunder.[4]

The Souls of Black Folk reveals a profound change in Dr. Du Bois' thinking. No longer did he believe that the so-called Negro Problem could be solved by a scientific attack upon white ignorance. Statements of truth based on scientific evidence would not bring reform. A new approach was needed in the fight against white oppression, and his approach would be an outspoken demand for civil rights: the right to vote, the right to justice under the law, the right to attend decent schools, and the right to work. The Doctor further urged that blacks organize themselves into an economic group that could control its own markets.

In January 1905 Dr. Du Bois' anger could no

longer be held in check. Whenever white leaders asked for a black for a specific position in political, educational, or civil service, Booker T. Washington alone had the power to say who could have it. But at the same time Mr. Washington would deny this opportunity for jobs to blacks who criticized his ideas. Now Dr. Du Bois publicly blasted the Tuskegee Machine. The militant black publication *Voice of the Negro,* edited by his close friend J. Max Barber, printed Dr. Du Bois' charge that some unnamed newspapers received $4,000 in "persuasion" or "hush money" in 1904. In Monroe Trotter's Boston *Guardian* the Doctor stated that sections of the black press had been paid to attack those who spoke out against Booker T. Washington.

Oswald Garrison Villard, the liberal editor of the *New York Evening Post* and grandson of abolitionist William Lloyd Garrison, asked the Doctor to prove his charges. *The New York Age,* the black newspaper for which the Doctor had distributed papers as a high school youth, called him a "Professor of Hysterics" and demanded that he tell the names of the newspapers who had received secret money. The editors of the *Voice of the Negro* also asked Dr. Du Bois for specific information.

Dr. Du Bois would make no further comment. But in letters to Oswald Villard and W. H. Ward, editor of the liberal, white-owned *Independent,* Dr. Du Bois wrote that the newspapers attacking him were the same ones that were getting paid to praise the Booker T. Washington program and the Tuskegee Machine. He found it "significant," he said, that the guilty papers "print the same syndicated news and praise the same persons and attack the same persons." (Washington appears to have rewarded his allies among the black newspapers financially, for in 1904 he secretly invested $3,000 in a magazine which supported him called the *Colored American*.[5])

Syndicated news and editorials were not so common in 1905, and to Dr. Du Bois and others such syndication seemed "monstrous and dishonest." However, many newspapers did sincerely share Mr. Washington's opinions, believing that emphasis on economics was the surest way to improve the conditions of blacks. Like Mr. Washington they believed that industrial education would allow black skilled workmen to take their rightful place in an industrial society. Higher education, the right to vote, even the battle for equality, were not nearly as important. These newspapers understood that Mr. Washington, because of his position as *leader*, had the white South closely watching his activities.

Nevertheless, there is evidence that Booker T. Washington did have a smooth and tightly controlled organization which watched the black press and influenced a large portion of it. There is also evidence that he feared intellectuals like William Du Bois and Monroe Trotter because he could not control them and because they had much more formal education than he had. And underlying the whole Du Bois–Washington controversy is a strange but very real conflict— the conflict of the black southerner at odds with the black northerner: the former slave versus the freeman. On Mr. Washington's side there was suspicion of the outsider coming along to tell the southerner how he should live his life. And working against Dr. Du Bois was his somewhat arrogant manner and his certainty that he knew what was best for his people.

Eventually there was a strong revolt within the black leadership against the Tuskegee Machine. In 1905 Dr. Du Bois invited some of his supporters to meet at the home of Kelly Miller, a graduate of Harvard and dean of Howard University's College of Arts and Sciences. The meeting was held for the purpose of forming a social-action committee. But in a few short weeks the demands of Dr. Du Bois and his associates would come into irrevocable conflict with Mr. Washington and his Tuskegee Machine.

CHAPTER 8

F ROM ATLANTA IN
June 1905 Dr. Du Bois sent out a call for a second
meeting. The call went to a few selected persons "for
organized determination and aggressive action on the
part of men who believe in Negro freedom and growth."
A July conference was held at Niagara Falls in a small
hotel hired for the purpose on the Canadian side. No
American hotel would accommodate the Talented
Tenth of black people. In all, twenty-nine men
from fourteen states answered the Doctor's call and
attended the meeting. The Doctor was elected general
secretary of what became known later as the Niagara
Movement. The platform of the 1905 session and the
Movement was written in a tone of toughness. The
radicals, as they became known, told the whites what
had to be done. They demanded complete political and
social equality and proclaimed their opposition to the
conservatives and to Booker T. Washington's appeasement policy.

As a national organization, the Niagara Movement demanded equal voting and civil rights for black people. It launched an attack on Jim Crow laws by bringing into court certain cases that would test their validity. A year after its formation the Movement successfully appealed the case of a young black woman who had been fined for refusing to enter a Jim Crow car on a train.

The Movement's "Declaration of Principles," written by Monroe Trotter and Dr. Du Bois, revealed the depth of the radical protest that was the basis of the Du Bois philosophy. The aim of the declaration was to make blacks indignant—angry enough to fight against injustice—and to offer them an alternative to the humble moderation of Booker T. Washington. It called for:

1. Freedom of speech and criticism.
2. An unfettered and unsubsidized press.
3. Manhood suffrage.
4. The abolition of all caste distinctions based simply on race and color.
5. The recognition of the principle of human brotherhood as a practical present creed.
6. The recognition of the highest and best human training as the monopoly of no class or race.
7. A belief in the dignity of labor.
8. United effort to realize these ideals under wise and courageous leadership.

The Niagara Movement brought down upon itself a torrent of criticism. Dr. Du Bois was accused of being

W. E. B. Du Bois in 1887 when he was a junior at Fisk

Dr. Du Bois at Wilberforce

*Dr. Du Bois (second row, second from the right)
and other leaders of the Niagara Movement at Fort
Erie, Canada, in 1905*

At his desk at Atlanta University in 1909

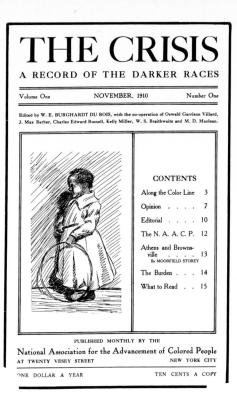

The front cover of the first issue of The Crisis

In the office of The Crisis

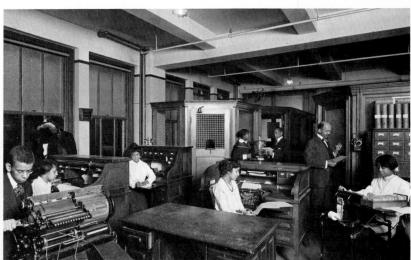

Dr. Du Bois circa 1920

*Dr. Du Bois (second row, second from the right) in 1917 in a parade spon-
sored by the N.A.A.C.P. to protest lynching in the United States*

At the wedding of Dr. Du Bois' daughter, Yolande (front row, second from the left) to Countee Cullen (second row, fifth from the left) in 1928. In the last row are Langston Hughes (second from the left) and Arna Bontemps (third from the left).

Dr. Du Bois in 1940

In 1950, when the Peace Information Center had been ordered by the Justice Department to register as an agent of a foreign principal

Dr. Du Bois in 1950 with Mary McLeod Bethune, the distinguished educator, and Horace Mann Bond, president of Lincoln University

In his library in 1956

At the Soviet Embassy in 1959, when he was presented with the Lenin Peace Prize. On Dr. Du Bois' right is his wife Shirley Graham Du Bois. Behind them is his daughter, Yolande.

Dr. Du Bois celebrates his ninety-fifth birthday in 1963 in Accra, Ghana. With him is the president of Ghana, Kwame Nkrumah.

ashamed of being black! Some said he had formed the Niagara Movement because he envied the leadership of Booker T. Washington. Mr. Washington himself believed that the radicals were fools and that Dr. Du Bois was simply jealous of him. Eventually he would try unsuccessfully to undermine and destroy the Niagara Movement by taking it over from within. Friends of both Dr. Du Bois and Mr. Washington tried, but failed, to bring the two together in understanding.

At its next meeting, in 1906 at Harper's Ferry, West Virginia, the scene of John Brown's raid, the Movement drew up resolutions that ended with these words:

> We do not believe in violence, neither in the despised violence of the raid nor the lauded violence of the soldier, nor the barbarous violence of the mob, but we do believe in John Brown, in that incarnate spirit of justice, that hatred of a lie, that willingness to sacrifice money, reputation, and life itself on the altar of right. And here on the scene of John Brown's martyrdom we reconsecrate ourselves, our honor, our property to the final emancipation of the race which John Brown died to make free.[1]

These extraordinary words hit home with sickening urgency when, in September 1906, the Atlanta Riot occurred.

Depriving blacks of their right to vote was the issue of a local Atlanta political campaign. Speeches by rabid segregationists and headlines and articles in the press stirred up the deep-felt southern hatred of blacks.

After months of such rabble-rousing, whites took to the streets of Atlanta, beating and killing blacks. When the blacks fought back in self-defense, uniformed police joined the white mobs. The *Voice of the Negro* publication was forced to close its office, and J. Max Barber, its editor, fled from Atlanta. By the end of the so-called riot—it was in fact a brutal attack by whites on the blacks—ten blacks and two whites were dead and scores more were wounded.

The deplorable atmosphere of hate in Atlanta before the violence is clearly reflected in a letter written by Mr. Barber on September 26, 1906, to the New York *World*. The letter was in answer to one already published in the *World* by John Temple Graves of the Atlanta *Georgian*. A section of the Barber letter reads:

Remember that Charles Daniel, Editor of the Atlanta *News,* had for more than a month sought by every hellish device to precipitate a race war. He had called for reorganization of the Ku Klux Klan, had offered a reward to lynchers, and had written daily fire-eating and reckless editorials against the Negro. Remember that Mr. Graves himself had written repeatedly in limpid and classic style about "The Shadow of the Black Terror." Remember that the Atlanta *Journal* had exhausted its vocabulary abusing the Negro, while the *Constitution* was mum. Then, finally, there came these extras with alarming rapidity on Saturday night with the headlines a foot deep.

There had to be some blood letting. There was some blood letting but the innocent were the only ones to suffer.

The cause of this riot: Sensational newspapers and unscrupulous politicians. The remedy: An impartial enforcement of the laws of the land. The authorities must protect the people. Although the newspapers have not said so, almost as many white people were killed and as many were wounded as colored in this riot.[2]

Dr. Du Bois was away in Alabama when the Atlanta Riot occurred, and, fearing that harm might come to his family, he hurried home. His daughter, Yolande, was six years old and the darling of the Atlanta University campus. Worried to death about the safety of Yolande, his wife, and his friends, he slept little on the train ride home. It was this night that he wrote a long, despairing poem entitled *A Litany at Atlanta:*

. . . Behold this maimed and broken thing, dear God; it was a humble black man, who toiled and sweat to save a bit from the pittance paid him. They told him: *Work and Rise.* He worked. Did this man sin? Nay, but someone told how someone said another did—one whom he had never seen nor known. Yet for that man's crime this man lieth maimed and murdered, his wife naked to shame, his children to poverty and evil . . . [3]

Du Bois soon attempted to found a magazine for blacks, an idea he had thought about for some time. In 1906 he began publishing a paper called *The Moon* but gave it up after a year. Then in 1907 he started a monthly magazine called *Horizon,* the official publication of the Niagara Movement.

The Niagara Movement had advocated a program of racial equality at a time in history when blacks were systematically excluded from social and political life. Its significance lay in the fact that it organized an articulate pressure group of citizens into the first political lobby of its kind among black people. The all-black Niagara Movement, using a strategy of protest, bravely attempted to counteract Booker T. Washington's philosophy of appeasement. But its membership had little money of its own, and it suffered because it was unable to attract wealthy whites. Its central aim was always political: Give blacks the right to vote. Unfortunately, the Movement confronted white supremacy in a period when the South was becoming ever more successful in disenfranchising its blacks. Through discrimination and intimidation, the South was limiting the black worker to menial labor and freezing his earning power at a poverty level.

The Niagara Movement limped along, but it was not a failure. For it returned to black America its age-old spirit of protest and battle—the spirit of the slave uprisings and revolts. Even when the cotton South had been king, white supremacy could never quite quell that spirit.

Without the power of money or the strength of numbers, the Niagara Movement had tried to force change upon the same system of master and slave which now, more than forty years after the Civil War, saw nothing wrong in using black labor as the brute upon whose back the South would rise again.

Mr. Washington and his Tuskegee Machine had the support of wealthy white friends and large segments of the black press who believed only in the words and wisdom of the Leader. The enormous power of the Machine supported the simplistic, blind philosophy of Booker T. Washington and made it common knowledge. As a means by which blacks might progress and prevail, the philosophy was at best an awful blunder. The Leader himself failed his people by fervently demanding that they who were daily humiliated and brutalized wait patiently for the master to give recognition to the slave. Mr. Washington believed in the basic goodwill of the white South; and thus, he did grave damage to the free spirit of his people for years to come.

When the end of the Niagara Movement was near at hand, a new committee was founded, in response to a terrible riot that occurred in 1908 at Springfield, Illinois. Two blacks were lynched during the riot, four whites were murdered, and seventy persons in all were injured. Blacks living through this awful time knew that there was nowhere they could live peacefully or sleep without fear. And in the minds of many reformers a permanent civil rights group was desperately needed to protect the freedom of blacks. In May 1909 a National Negro Committee gathered in New York City; composed of both whites and blacks, it stood for racial equality.

This 1909 conference attracted scientists, philanthropists, and social workers for a new crusade, but there were few followers of Booker T. Washington.

One of the delegates, Oswald Garrison Villard, had formerly had complete faith in Mr. Washington but had become disturbed by his leadership. Mr. Villard believed also that William Howard Taft, who had defeated William Jennings Bryan for president in 1908, ignored the real injustices done to black people. Mr. Villard joined the National Negro Committee along with other white reformers, including Jane Addams and Lincoln Steffens.

The next year, the name of the National Negro Committee was formally changed to the National Association for the Advancement of Colored People, thereafter usually referred to as the Association or the NAACP.

From the first, the whites in the NAACP held the topmost administrative positions. When the Constitutional League, a civil rights organization, merged with the NAACP, John E. Milholland, its president, became vice-president of the NAACP.

The blacks in the NAACP included Dr. Du Bois; Francis J. Grimké; Alexander Walters, bishop of the African Episcopal Church and president of the Afro-American Council; and Dr. J. Milton Waldron, former treasurer of the Niagara Movement. Monroe Trotter and Ida Wells Barnett, the crusader against lynching, refused to join. They were the most radical of the black leadership and distrusted the whites in the newly formed group.

Dr. Du Bois was the only black administrator in the

list of officers of the NAACP. He had been asked to take the position of Director of Publications and Research and had accepted the post. In 1910 he left Atlanta University. The publication of the Atlanta studies in 1914 marked the end of his connection with the university for the next twenty years.

Much later, Dr. Du Bois wrote in his autobiography somewhat sadly:

> My career as a scientist was to be swallowed up in my role as master of propaganda. This was not wholly to my liking. I was no natural leader of men . . . . Nevertheless, having put my hand to the plow, I had to go on. The Niagara Movement . . . began to suffer internal strain from the dynamic personality of [Monroe] Trotter and my own inexperience with organizations. Finally, it practically became merged with a new and enveloping organization of which I became a leading official—the National Association for the Advancement of Colored People.[4]

The NAACP started as a single, national office which released statements to the public on matters affecting blacks. As its membership grew, NAACP branches developed across the country.

The aim of the NAACP was black equality with white America. It focused its activity on discrimination and segregation, with education, legal action, and organization as weapons for the attack. The Association intended to educate the American people in an understanding of the abuses of Negro rights. It would make appeals for blacks in court and before legislatures. Lastly, the Association itself would be a close-knit group of articulate citizens, both black and white, who believed true democracy was possible in the United States.

The NAACP made the assumption, as had Dr. Du Bois earlier, that from the moment Americans knew of injustice to blacks, they would demand reform from the government.

Once NAACP branches had been established, a division of labor developed between the national office in New York and these branches. The branches sent information into the New York headquarters. Material prepared at headquarters went out to the branches for distribution to the people. The national office handled national questions, and the branches dealt with local matters. All focused on the spread of information concerning the civil rights of black Americans.

One weakness of the radicals when organized into the all-black Niagara Movement had been their inability to attract white support. Now Dr. Du Bois and other radicals willingly became a part of the NAACP because they thought that the support of white liberal reformers in the Association, who believed in personal and equal justice for all, would enable them to realize their aims. It was unfortunately true then, as it is today, that an all-black organization found the going difficult; indeed, such an organization was often looked on with suspicion, not only by whites but by blacks as well, if it did not have the approval and active support of white liberal opinion.

The white reformers of the NAACP had enough money to develop a solid protest organization and enough faith in democratic rule to associate themselves with Dr. Du Bois' black radical thought. The Doctor himself was concerned about the relationship between the white liberal reformers, who were aligned with the labor movement in America and the black radicals, whom he called "the American Negro group."

He wrote: "Back of this lay an unasked question as to the relation of the American Negro group to the whole labor movement. This was not yet raised but several of the group were socialists, including myself."

Dr. Du Bois joined the Socialist Party in 1911. He desired government ownership of basic industry while remaining suspicious of white workers, who, he felt, discriminated against blacks. There were some white socialists among the reformers of the NAACP, and their alliance with black radicals was a unique, imaginative vote of confidence in American democracy.

During the period of the formation of the NAACP, the Doctor was traveling and lecturing widely. He was also writing books. His biography of John Brown— who had attempted to seize the federal arsenal at Harper's Ferry in order to arm the slaves—had been published in 1909. Dr. Du Bois considered *John Brown* the best written of his works. In this book, he had raised the now-familiar question of whether a peaceful solution of grave problems could be obtained by means of violence.

In 1911 he published *The Quest of the Silver Fleece,* a work of fiction concerned with freedom for blacks. Other books followed: *The Negro,* published in 1915; *Darkwater: Voices From Within The Veil,* in 1920; *The Gift of Black Folk: Negroes in the Making of America,* in 1924; *Dark Princess: A Romance,* in 1928; and *Black Reconstruction in America 1860–1880,* in 1935.

Even though Dr. Du Bois wrote constantly, he considered his life from 1910 to 1934 to be mainly the story of *The Crisis* magazine.

As Director of Research and Publications, Dr. Du Bois was a member of the Board of Directors of the NAACP. As yet, no funds were available for research, although as his title indicates, half of his job was supposed to be devoted to it. The Doctor conceived and founded *The Crisis,* and most of his time was spent editing and publishing it. The magazine became immediately important as the NAACP's official publication. In it Dr. Du Bois wrote about all aspects of black life in America. His first editorial, published in November 1910, stated the aim of the magazine:

The policy of *The Crisis* will be simple and well defined:

It will first and foremost be a newspaper: it will

record important happenings and movements in the
world which bear on the great problems of inter-racial
relations. . . .

Secondly, it will be a review of opinion and literature, recording briefly books, articles, and important
expressions of opinion in the white and colored press
on the race problem.

Thirdly, it will publish a few short articles.

Finally, its editorial page will stand for the rights
of men, irrespective of color or race, for the highest
ideals of American democracy, and for reasonable
but earnest and persistent attempt to gain these rights
and realize these ideals. The magazine will be the
organ of no clique or party and will avoid personal
rancor of all sorts. In the absence of proof to the con-
trary it will assume honesty of purpose on the part of
all men, North and South, white and black.

Through *The Crisis,* Dr. Du Bois supported and
took note of the work of the NAACP. Joel Spingarn,
the chairman of the NAACP, suggested that the editorials written by the Doctor should be an expression
of his own mind and personality. And for twenty years
the opinion of Dr. Du Bois and his *Crisis* and that of
the NAACP were generally the same. However, from
the beginning, the Doctor began developing a point of
view toward black economic self-sufficiency independent of the thinking of the Association.

The NAACP met with difficulty when trying to
evolve an attitude toward Booker T. Washington. In
America in 1910 it was impossible to discuss black

problems without in some way bringing up his name. At the time he was in Europe making speeches in which he said that the so-called Negro Problem in America was on the way to being solved. Obviously this was not true, and Dr. Du Bois said as much in a document issued by the National Negro Committee in October 1910:

> [Mr. Washington] is a distinguished American and has a perfect right to his opinions. But we are compelled to point out that Mr. Washington's large financial responsibilities have made him dependent on the rich charitable public and that, for this reason, he has for years been compelled to tell, not the whole truth, but that part of it which certain powerful interests in America wished to appear as the whole truth.[5]

This statement brought an immediate reaction from *The Raleigh News and Courier,* which Dr. Du Bois reprinted in *The Crisis:*

> It is hard to tell which is the worse enemy of the Negro race—the brute who invites lynching by the basest of crimes, or the social-equality-hunting fellow like Du Bois, who slanders his country. Fortunately for the peaceable and industrious Negroes in the South, the world does not judge them either by Du Bois or the animal, and helps them and is in sympathy with their efforts to better their conditions.

Other publications, such as the *Philadelphia Bulletin,* brought up the old accusation that Dr. Du Bois' fight for equality was nothing more than a desire on his part to be white.

In *The Crisis* the Doctor wrote that he was not asking for special treatment for blacks but simply for an equal chance. In this, he and the Association agreed. Basically the NAACP sought to rid the country of barriers that held black citizens back from reaching their highest level of accomplishment. The group focused on all phases of discrimination and proposed a program of education and legal action to fight it. However, Dr. Du Bois looked beyond the program of an interracial group tearing down obstacles of oppression whenever these were raised. As a black man, he was not fighting merely for the strength and the patience to endure the color line. He believed he must find aggressive means by which blacks would be able to surmount entrenched color prejudice.

The relationship between Dr. Du Bois and his white liberal colleagues on the NAACP board grew difficult at times, but it held. The Association had no intention of losing the Doctor's fantastic ability as the editor of its ever more successful magazine. His reputation as a scholar, lecturer, critic, and literary figure grew daily. He attended the Universal Races Congress in London in 1911. The Congress, called by the Ethical Culture Societies of the world, was the first international and interracial forum of scientists devoted to social reform and racial equality. That a distinguished member of the NAACP board was asked to address the Congress further enhanced the prestige of the Association.

At the Congress Dr. Du Bois stressed the NAACP position on the need for racial equality and for a firm fight against segregation. He had stated in 1907 that he didn't believe in physical segregation of races, but that it was possible for blacks to remain involved with whites while buying from their own markets and department stores. Now, going beyond the NAACP program, he began to emphasize more economic separation by blacks for their own survival during the time the race was fighting prejudice through legal means and intelligent action.

The circulation of *The Crisis* grew from 1,000 copies a month in 1910 to 30,000 in 1913, and the growth demonstrates an important change among black people in their attitude toward themselves in relation to the rest of America.

Booker T. Washington had delivered his Atlanta Compromise speech in 1895, when every third southerner was a black man and when the usual black was a poor southerner and a poor farmer. He had told these blacks to "Cast down your bucket where you are," at a time where there seemed little chance for them to escape the South. He had spoken what he felt he must to a trapped people, if they were to endure their dreadful ordeal.

By 1915 the South had changed, for the boll weevil from Mexico had devastated southern cotton fields by the thousands. This onslaught, plus drought and floods, forced the poor black tenant farmers to search for other work. The North was short of unskilled laborers because World War I, which had started in 1914, had cut off the migration of European immigrants to America. Northern industry began to send agents to the South to recruit black workers. Blacks were pulled from the farms to the cities of the North in large numbers. And in no time this black migration hit the North like a tidal wave, for in one year in the five-year period between 1915 and 1920, half a million blacks had moved north. Gathering into ever more crowded "darktowns" and "ghettos," these new city blacks found that they could now protect one another and they could vote. Neither had been possible in the South.

The new city blacks soon found that northern whites viewed their migration literally as an attack on themselves. They fought to keep the blacks from obtaining skilled jobs and from living in their communities, both through legal means and open violence. Such discrimination and prejudice in the North soon made the new city blacks responsive to the radical political views of Dr. Du Bois' *Crisis* editorials:

Take, for instance, the question of the intermarrying of white and black folk; it is a question that colored people seldom discuss. It is about the last of the social problems over which they are disturbed, because they so seldom face it in fact or in theory. Their problems are problems of work and wages, of the right to vote, of the right to travel decently, of the right to frequent places of public amusement, of the right to public security.

White people, on the other hand, for the most part profess to see but one problem: "Do you want your sister to marry a nigger?" . . .

For the thousands of new city blacks the Washington philosophy of compromise and moderation gradually lost its appeal, and the power of the Tuskegee Machine slowly diminished. *The Crisis* and the militant position of Dr. Du Bois offered to hopeful black populations a confirmation of black suffering:

. . . for the great mass of 10,000,000 Americans of Negro descent these things are true:

We are denied education.

We are driven out of the Church of Christ.

We are forced out of hotels, theaters and public places.

We are publicly labeled like dogs when we travel.

We can seldom get decent employment.

We are forced down to the lowest wage scale.

We pay the highest rent for the poorest homes.

We cannot buy property in decent neighborhoods.

We are held up to ridicule in the press and on the platform and stage.

We are disfranchised.

We are taxed without representation.

We are denied the right to choose our friends or to be chosen by them. . . .

In law and custom our women have no rights which a white man is bound to respect.

We cannot get justice in the courts.

We are lynched with impunity.

We are publicly, continuously and shamefully insulted from the day of our birth to the day of our death.

And yet we are told not to be "self conscious," to lie about the truth in order to make it "come true"; to grapple with the "philosophy of evolution"; and not to make people "feel ugly" by telling them "ugly facts". . . .

The list of insults to blacks printed in the above *Crisis* editorial in 1914 hits the eye with chilling recognition. For many of the insults remain facts of black life in America today.

Month after month *The Crisis* reached the NAACP branches and black neighborhoods. The opinions of its editor—"If we are to die, in God's name let us perish like men and not like bales of hay"—became in the minds of black Americans truly the voice of the NAACP and the "soul of black folk." For the conditions the Doctor had written about in 1903 in *The Souls of Black Folk* remained the same in 1915: "the problem of the Twentieth Century is the problem of the color line."

The gifted ex-slave and president of Tuskegee Institute, Booker T. Washington, died in 1915. Dr. W. E. Burghardt Du Bois then became the outstanding leader of black people.

CHAPTER 9

W ILLIAM HOW-
ard Taft and Theodore Roosevelt, both presidential
candidates in the election of 1912, found that black
voters were deserting them. The ever more sophisticated
black electorate was moving toward an independent
attitude in politics. The Republican, William Howard
Taft, had told the blacks that they should stay content
with being farmers. Running on the Progressive party
ticket, Theodore Roosevelt excluded black men from
some of the southern delegations to the party's national
convention.

As early as 1908 Dr. Du Bois, angry at Theodore
Roosevelt's and William Howard Taft's obvious dis-
regard for black people, had written these words:

> . . . It would be well for thoughtful colored citizens
> to sit down a while before election and do some hard
> thinking.
> We have been voting for forty years on the theory
> that Republicans freed the race from slavery and

Democrats are responsible for southern prejudices.
Is this true? The Republican party never intended
to free the slaves. It never began the war with any
such idea. It was willing to end the war and not touch
slavery. . . .[1]

Searching for a position from which they might successfully fight for their just cause, some black leaders
began to look to the Socialist Party of America. The
doctrine of socialism was based on the equality of all
mankind, and the party refused to separate the particu-
lar oppression of the entire black race from the exploitation of workers in general. Nonetheless, blacks
began to listen when the Socialist leader, Eugene V.
Debs, stated that the Socialist party was the hope and
friend of blacks.

Dr. Du Bois already had begun to see the question of
black rights as a problem of oppressed workers, black
and white. And in 1907 he had written in *Horizon:*

I am a Socialist-of-the-Path. I do not believe in the
complete socialization of the means of production—
the entire abolition of private property in capital—
but the Path of Progress and common sense certainly
leads to a far greater ownership of the public wealth
for the public good than is now the case. I do not believe that government can carry on private business as
well as private concerns, but I do believe that most of
the human business called private is no more private
than God's blue sky, and that we are approaching a time
when railroads, coal mines and many factories can

and ought to be run by the public for the public. This is the way, as I see it, that the path leads and I follow it gladly and hopefully.[2]

In other words, the position of Dr. Du Bois and other race leaders was that they would support any political party which declared itself on the side of blacks in their fight for equal justice.

Woodrow Wilson, a southerner and the president of Princeton University, entered the presidential arena of 1912 as the candidate of the Democratic party. In his campaign he told black people that "they may count upon me for absolute fair dealing," and "for everything by which I could assist in advancing the interests of their race."

Now Dr. Du Bois believed that at last there was a candidate who cared about the grievances of blacks. He therefore committed himself to support Mr. Wilson's bid for election. The Doctor did not give up his Socialist leanings, but felt, rather, that for him to urge blacks to support the Socialist party ticket, which generally won only a small percentage of votes in national elections, would be asking them to throw their votes away.

The Doctor resigned from New York Local #1 of the Socialist party, which he had joined in 1911. He then threw the weight of *The Crisis,* which by 1912 had a national following, behind the election of Woodrow Wilson. Bishop Alexander Walters of the African Zion Church had secured a statement from Mr. Wilson in which he expressed an "earnest wish to see justice done the colored people in every matter."

William Howard Taft and Theodore Roosevelt split the Republican vote in 1912, and Woodrow Wilson was elected president of the United States. Mr. Wilson's slogan was "New Freedom" for America; both black and white voters waited eagerly for that freedom.

But soon black Americans found out that this New Freedom was no better than empty words. In the first year of the Wilson administration Congress proposed legislation against blacks which had never before been introduced. Twenty bills advocated Jim Crow cars on trains in Washington, D.C. There were bills which recommended segregation of federal employees, the exclusion of blacks from commissions in the army and navy, a ban on white-black intermarriage, and the exclusion from America of immigrants of African descent.

The NAACP now fought not only against lynching and discrimination, but against this shocking legislation proposed in Congress. Most of the bills never saw the light of day. But one was enacted by President Wilson's executive order: All black federal employees were to be segregated into separate work rooms with separate eating and toilet facilities.

A group of black leaders led by Monroe Trotter paid a visit to President Wilson in 1913 and again in 1914, protesting the segregation of government employees. But in the president's view, such segregation would ease racial friction between blacks and whites. The president told the black leaders, "Segregation is not humiliating but a benefit, and ought to be so regarded by you gentlemen."

When Monroe Trotter persisted, pointing out to the president that blacks and whites had worked together for half a century, Mr. Wilson became angry and called Mr. Trotter's language insulting. Monroe Trotter was furious, and it was clear to him that the President of the United States had no intention of changing his policy.

This was a sad time for black Americans. As usual, they found that they had to depend upon themselves, accepting only the support of whites who could prove they were trustworthy.

A year after the death of Booker T. Washington the chairman of the NAACP board, Joel Spingarn, called two hundred black leaders to a "peace conference" at his summer home in Amenia, New York. Now that Mr. Washington was dead, the group found they had little to fight about. The Amenia Conference adopted a body of resolutions pledging to fight for complete civil rights for blacks. They resolved that blacks must have political freedom in order to reach their highest level of political development. Furthermore, blacks must have the right to all forms of education, not merely industrial education.

The unity shown at Amenia reflected important changes in the thinking of black leaders. Their resolutions, largely written by Dr. Du Bois but accepted by all the participants at the conference, displayed none of the humility toward whites of the Washington philosophy.

Month upon month *The Crisis* continued to influence blacks as well as whites. Its editorials were mentioned in Congress, and no other black leader spoke with the authority of Dr. Du Bois. However, black life in America had become too complex for one man to act as the sole spokesman for all blacks. One leader had been possible before the great black exodus from the South, when a man such as Mr. Washington had "led" his people. But with black people now settled in the teeming ghettoes of the North, there were black leaders on the local level who could work for the people street by street and effect change in neighborhoods through local political strength.

But the fact remained that no other man could reach a national audience and produce a general change in black attitudes the way Dr. Du Bois did with his *Crisis,* as shown in this excerpt from his writing in 1914:

> As a race we are still kept in ignorance far below the average standard of this nation and of the present age, and the ideals set before our children in most cases are far below their possibilities and reasonable promise.
>
> This is true not by accident but by design, and by the design not so much of the laboring white masses of the nation but rather by the design of rich and intelligent people, and particularly by those who mas-

querade as the Negroes' "friends." Their attack on real education for Negroes is in reality one with their attack on education for working men in general and this is part of the great modern attack upon democracy. . . . In all these . . . actions there blazes one great and shining light: the persistent army of Negro boys and girls pushing through high school and college continues to increase. Negro mothers and fathers are not being entirely deceived. They know that intelligence and self-development are the only means by which the Negro is to win his way in the modern world. They persist in pushing their children on through the highest courses. May they always continue to do so; and may the Negro students in the coming years resist the contemptible temptation so persistently laid before this race to train its children simply as menials and scavengers.

Soon after Woodrow Wilson's election, World War I broke out, bringing prosperity to northern cities, where most of the factories of America were located. And from 1910 to 1920 one million blacks moved from the South to the North seeking better jobs and homes and a measure of freedom from discrimination. But there came a sudden increase of lynchings and harsher efforts at segregation as black people swelled the population of the cities.

In 1916 Dr. Du Bois refused to continue supporting President Wilson, who had brought segregation into the departments of the U.S. Post Office and Treasury, among others, and who had done nothing to stem the tide of lynchings. The Doctor urged blacks to vote for the Socialist presidential candidate, Allen L. Benson. If the candidates of the major parties refused to support the bid of blacks for equality, then the blacks should deny them their votes. The Socialists were openly against America entering the war in Europe, which they considered a "crime" committed by capitalists. The United States Congress, fearing that the Socialists' views might spread throughout the population, passed a series of laws to stifle such antiwar, anticapitalist opinion.

The Espionage Act of June 1917 imposed harsh punishment for disloyalty in the armed forces and for deliberate attempts to obstruct recruitment of soldiers. Under the Act, the postmaster-general was instructed to bar from the mails any material thought to promote discontent.

Eugene V. Debs, five times the Socialist party presidential candidate, was sentenced to ten years in prison for opposing America's involvement in the war. Soon after the 1917 Communist Revolution in Russia, any person in America with liberal or radical ideas was looked on as a dangerous "subversive."

At the beginning of the war the United States government refused to allow blacks to volunteer for the army. When the drafting of troops began in May 1917, racial segregation in the armed forces was written into law. Blacks would be drafted, but they would have to be trained separately from whites. Eighty-three thousand black draftees went into separate units in separate camps.

The federal government had to dismiss the Atlanta

Draft Board in a body for open race discrimination: literally hundreds of blacks were drafted without regard for their physical condition or their duties to their families.

Now the NAACP fought against the indecent treatment of black draftees. It fought to make certain that black draftees were not forced to do hard labor but were allowed to perform the same military functions as the whites. Above all, the NAACP wanted to be sure that some blacks became commissioned officers. If there were to be black officers, there would have to be, under the law, segregated officer-training camps. Joel Spingarn of the NAACP board believed it necessary that blacks prove to whites that they could handle leadership. He recommended the establishment of a segregated officer-candidate school, knowing that the army would never permit blacks to be trained at white officer schools.

The Boston *Guardian* and the Chicago *Defender* urged the NAACP not to accept a segregated officer camp. Mr. Spingarn offered to resign as chairman of the NAACP board so that the Association would not be embarrassed by his proposal. Dr. Du Bois supported Mr. Spingarn in *The Crisis,* for he felt that Mr. Spingarn and himself were caught in what he called the "Perpetual Dilemma." The evil of segregation was a fact of black life. There were black schools, black housing areas, black churches—on and on. If blacks did not acknowledge segregation now, Dr. Du Bois believed, they would get nothing from the whites.

The Doctor was charged with selling out to the whites; and hurt by the clamor of voices raised against him, he wrote in *The Crisis* in 1917:

Where in heaven's name do we Negroes stand? If we organize separately for anything—"Jim Crow!" scream all the Disconsolate; if we organize with white people—"Traitors! Pressure! They're betraying us!" yell all the Suspicious. If, unable to get the whole loaf we seize half to ward off starvation—"Compromise!" yell all the Scared. If we let the half loaf go and starve—"Why don't you *do* something?" yell those same critics, dancing about on their toes.

Finally an all-black officer-training camp was established at Des Moines, Iowa, in May 1917. Many black leaders doubted if any of the men would ever receive their commissions, especially after Dr. Du Bois tried unsuccessfully to see the secretary of war, Newton Baker. By late summer a number of the officer candidates were preparing to leave the Des Moines camp. But then Dr. Du Bois was permitted to see Secretary Baker, who rather coldly informed him that the country wasn't fighting a war only to find a solution to the black man's problems. The Doctor answered that a successful outcome of the war waged, in Woodrow Wilson's words, "to make the world safe for Democracy," might be thwarted by racism. Very soon after this meeting hundreds of black men received their commissions as officers in the U.S. Army.

The *Messenger* magazine began publication in 1917,

with Chandler Owen and A. Philip Randolph as its editors. They represented a new breed of the black Talented Tenth, and they felt that Dr. Du Bois, who was approaching fifty, was old-fashioned and conservative. The *Messenger* accused the Doctor of having an antilabor record and of turning away from his former aim of integration to support segregation. As had happened before, the public misunderstood the Doctor. His immediate goal was some measure of security for blacks, while at the same time his long-range goal of integration was being pursued.

In early 1918, after thirteen members of the 24th Infantry Regiment were hanged for their involvement in the Houston race riot of the preceding year, Dr. Du Bois once again condemned the conditions in America that black people were forced to endure. The U.S. Department of Justice cautioned the NAACP that the Doctor's statements were harming the war effort. New legislation under consideration, it said, would make such statements illegal. Thus the NAACP board found it necessary to have the Doctor clear everything he wished published in *The Crisis* through the Association's legal consultant.

In May 1918 the Sedition Act was passed, with increased penalties for "disloyal or abusive language" directed at the United States government, the United States Constitution, or the United States flag. Any alien who believed in or advocated the forcible overthrow of the government, or who belonged to organizations expressing such views, could be deported.

But slowly Dr. Du Bois warmed to the war effort when he saw black soldiers being trained as officers, and an increase in black employment and wages at home. He thought that conditions for blacks were perhaps changing at last. And in the summer of 1918 he published an editorial in *The Crisis* that created a storm of protest among the black leadership. The editorial was entitled "Close Ranks." Perhaps naively it stated that victory in the war was the most important consideration for all Americans, and particularly for blacks, who by serving their country would have to be given justice in return: "Let us, while this war lasts, forget our special grievances and close ranks shoulder to shoulder with our fellow citizens and the allied nations that are fighting for democracy. We make no ordinary sacrifice, but we make it gladly and willingly with our eyes lifted to the hills."

The *Messenger,* highly incensed by "Close Ranks," said it would rather make Georgia safe for the Negro.

After the "storm," Dr. Du Bois found himself in the "eye of the hurricane." He was offered a commission in the United States Army Intelligence. The Washington branch of the NAACP thought that if the Doctor joined the army, he had better leave *The Crisis*. The Washington *Eagle* congratulated "Captain Du Bois on his choice of Army life."

Joel Spingarn had persuaded Dr. Du Bois to seek the commission and began to think again about resigning as NAACP Board Chairman. However, the army soon decided it was no longer interested in the Doctor as an intelligence officer. The idea had created too much criticism.

Since there were more jobs and higher wages for blacks than ever before, Dr. Du Bois continued his strategy of patriotism throughout the war. His position saddened many black leaders, who couldn't understand that he had long accepted segregation as a necessary tactic in some instances.

Throughout this period, Dr. Du Bois was traveling and lecturing widely. As testimony to his continuing fight for black equality, he encouraged the emigration of black people from the South, supported voting rights for women, and prized the "new rush of young blacks to college."

At the request of the NAACP, he went to Europe to investigate the racist treatment of black American soldiers. His findings there created a sensation, for he discovered a French military directive warning Frenchmen against being too friendly with these blacks. Segregationist interests in the American army had made the directive possible. It was addressed to the "French Military Mission stationed with the American Army" and was headed, "August 7, 1918. Secret information concerning the Black American Troops." Issued by the American Higher Command and reprinted in *The Crisis*, in May 1919, the directive said in part:

It is important for French officers who have been called upon to exercise command over black American troops, or to live in close contact with them, to have an exact idea of the position occupied by Negroes in the United States. . . . The increasing number of Negroes in the U.S. (about 15,000,000) would create for the white race in the Republic a menace of degeneracy were it not that an impassable gulf has been made between them. As this danger does not exist for the French race, the French public has become accustomed to treating the Negro with familiarity and indulgence.

This indulgence and this familiarity . . . are matters of grievous concern to the Americans. They consider them an affront to their national policy. . . .[3]

The publication of this directive so terrified southern congressmen that they succeeded in having the issue of *The Crisis* in which it appeared withheld from the mails for a time. Nonetheless, the directive revealed once again that southern whites, northern whites, and the United States government were willing to work together to discriminate against blacks.

World War I came to an end in November 1918. One hundred thousand black American soldiers had served overseas in Europe. The all-black 369th Regiment did not lose a foot of ground or a single prisoner in 191 days in combat. The all-black 371st Regiment won 121 French and 27 American Distinguished Service Crosses.[4]

In 1919 these soldiers returned home to the cheers of thousands of Americans as they passed in review down New York City's Fifth Avenue. But not long after the parades ended, the blacks who had defended their country as soldiers would have to defend themselves as civilians. As they demanded for themselves the democracy they had fought to save, ignorant as well as supposedly educated whites became afraid and decided that they must keep the black soldiers in their place. There then began one of the most intense racial rivalries ever witnessed in the United States. By the summer of 1919 there was rioting in Illinois, Nebraska, Texas, Arkansas, and Washington, D.C. Blacks riding peacefully on streetcars were suddenly set upon by white mobs and dragged off. Blacks strolling on the streets were beaten senseless on the sidewalks. Dining in their homes, blacks were attacked by mobs who burned crosses on their lawns.

The NAACP worked long and hard providing lawyers to defend abused and bloodied blacks. The Association brought the facts of lynch mobs and the Ku Klux Klan to the American public. The Klan was a powerful force in the United States during and after the war, with its hate campaign directed not only at blacks, but at Catholics, Jews, Orientals, labor union leaders, and so-called radicals of all types. Klan membership was estimated at five million, and the burning cross, that crude symbol of the Klan's displeasure, was said to flame from New York to Oregon as well as in the South. No President of the United States spoke out forcefully against the Klan during the whole period of postwar adjustment in America.

Fear and suspicion of racial and political minority groups by the white majority in the United States spread rapidly after World War I. In 1919 the Worker's party (later called the Communist party) was established in the United States. Congress slowed down immigration of foreigners into the country, and those who were able to gain admission were called "hyphenated Americans."

The Department of Justice under Attorney General A. Mitchell Palmer carried out mass arrests of political and labor "agitators." In one single raid government agents swooped down on 33 cities and arrested 2,700 individuals.

Attorney General Palmer soon began looking for "Radicalism and Sedition Among the Negroes" in black periodicals and newspapers. State and federal agents "invaded" the NAACP main office and the offices of *The Crisis*. They asked, "Just what, after all, are your objectives and activities?"

Dr. Du Bois had the satisfaction of sitting back in his chair and answering, "We are seeking to have the Constitution of the United States thoroughly and completely enforced."

Radical programs to counteract government oppression of minorities sprang up around the country. The most successful of these was the one launched by the black Jamaican Marcus Garvey. In his newspaper, *The Negro World,* and in his speeches Mr. Garvey spoke passionately of the black man's need for pride in his race. Blacks must choose their own leaders from the black masses, he said, and they would never be free until they had all returned to Africa.

Dr. Du Bois, too, raised his passionate voice. Furious that black soldiers should return to America to such brutal conditions, he wrote a blistering editorial in *The Crisis* in May 1919:

> . . . We return from the slavery of uniform which the world's madness demanded us to don to the freedom of civil garb. We stand again to look America squarely in the face and call a spade a spade. We sing: This country of ours, despite all its better souls have done and dreamed, is yet a shameful land.
>
> It lynches. . . .
> It disfranchises its own citizens. . . . It *steals* from us. It insults us. . . .
> This is the country to which we Soldiers of Democracy return.
>
> We *return*.
> We *return from fighting*.
> We *return fighting*.
>
> Make way for Democracy! We saved it in France, and by the Great Jehovah, we will save it in the United States of America, or know the reason why.

CHAPTER 10

THE YEARS FROM 1918
to 1928 were a time of hard, endless work for Dr.
William Du Bois. He was nervous, restless; he traveled
from the east coast to the west coast, north and south,
giving lectures and holding conferences. The Doctor
later wrote of this time: "I had to be a part of the
revolution through which the world was going and to
feel in my own soul the scars of its battle."

While in Europe in 1918 investigating the treatment
of black soldiers for the NAACP, Dr. Du Bois, at the
"behest of a group of American Negroes," decided
that Africa ought to be represented during the peace
efforts following the war. Actually, the Doctor had already conceived, and the NAACP had adopted, a program which proposed three goals for German, Belgian,
and French colonies in Africa, to be presented at the
Paris peace conference. Thus the NAACP and Dr. Du
Bois began to crusade for a free Africa. Dr. Du Bois was
further authorized by the Association to organize a

"Pan-African Congress" to help influence public opinion in favor of the program for an Africa free of colonial rule and to gain the attention of peace conference delegates and the world.

With the cooperation of Blaise Diagne, the French deputy from Senegal, Dr. Du Bois succeeded in gathering a Pan-African Congress at the Grand Hotel in Paris. There were fifty-seven delegates in all; they were American blacks, West Indians, and Africans. France, Belgium, and Portugal were represented by officials, and it was the first time that blacks from the American South had talked with blacks from Africa. A second Pan-African Congress was held in London, Paris, and Brussels in 1921, and a third in London, Paris, and Lisbon in 1923.

The Pan-African Congresses were serious, well-planned conclaves which advocated programs to unite Africa for black Africans. Talked about all over Europe, the congresses were rarely mentioned in the press of the United States. They were considered dangerous by imperialists who wished to exploit the resources of Africa, and in order to undermine pan-African goals, they were deliberately confused with the movement launched by Marcus Garvey. Mr. Garvey had come to America after the war to begin his plan for bringing together black groups and to develop "eventual black domination of Africa." Within a few short years his plans and dreams were known everywhere. He held huge conventions in New York and announced himself to the public as "the Provisional President of Africa."

He toured the United States, calling for an exodus of black people to Africa. The fall of 1920 saw fifty thousand Garvey followers parade through Harlem. Marcus Garvey led the parade dressed in his uniform of green, purple, and black with gold braid, and a hat with white plumes.

Dr. Du Bois has written that he at first tried to "explain away" the Garvey movement, to "ignore it . . ., but it was a mass movement that could not be ignored. I noted this movement from time to time in *The Crisis* and said in 1920 that Garvey was 'an extraordinary leader of men' and declared that he had 'with singular success capitalized and made vocal the great and long-suffering grievances and spirit of protest among the West Indian peasantry.' "

However, Dr. Du Bois believed it necessary for blacks on every continent to find their own solutions to oppression in their own countries. Black Americans could not possibly return to Africa, but must solve their problems at home. The basis for pan-Africanism and the congresses the Doctor had organized had been the concept that oppressed Africans had every right to run their own countries. Unfortunately for him and for his cause, the Garvey Movement was attracting hundreds of thousands of black people while his Pan-African Congresses came and went, virtually unnoticed at home.

Marcus Garvey ran afoul of American authorities when investors in his back-to-Africa Black Star Steamship line accused him of fraud. Garvey was indicted, brought to trial, and convicted of using the mails to defraud. He was sent to the Federal Penitentiary in Atlanta, Georgia, in 1925. After two years in prison he was pardoned by President Calvin Coolidge and deported to Jamaica.

Perhaps, in 1923, the extraordinary sense of self that Marcus Garvey gave to black people was all that could have been hoped for. Dr. Du Bois' Pan-African Congresses were far removed from race riots and the Ku Klux Klan. Marcus Garvey was able to make black people at home proud of their race and interested in knowing more about their African past. Garvey's finest contribution was that he aroused the hopes and dreams of rural southern blacks who had hastened to northern and midwestern urban areas after World War I.

At the war's end the NAACP mounted a campaign to publicize racial injustices among these immigrants from the South and to arouse public opinion in favor of justice and reform. In a far more concentrated program, the Association worked through the Congress of the United States, state legislatures, and the federal court system. Its Tenth Annual Report in 1920 revealed what would be the philosophy of the organization for the next forty years: The NAACP is interracial, and the separate-but-equal doctrine of the South is by its very nature unequal.[1]

Thus, the NAACP by 1920 had committed itself to protest with a policy calling for the integration of blacks into all phases of American society.

Dr. Du Bois was beginning to feel that economic and social equality could not be gained in America for blacks as long as the majority of whites were against it. He understood now that the cause of race prejudice went far beyond "ignorance and deliberate ill-will." There were stronger, more profound causes, perhaps, which had not yet been attacked. There were deep-seated feelings of superiority among whites, which had sunk to an unconscious level. These feelings came to the surface in the form of unshakable prejudice and an irrational fear of blacks. It was the Doctor's belief that blacks must now lead the attack on these hidden forces and cease merely to defend themselves as they had done in the past.

Dr. Du Bois had tried, through social reform and the scientific investigation of social problems, to bring about a truly interracial culture in the United States. But as America grew day by day more racially bitter, he became more socialist in his outlook and began to discuss publicly the importance of a planned black economy. He also championed the need for black control of civil rights organizations like the NAACP. In April 1915 he had written an article in *The Crisis* called "The Immediate Program of the American Negro," in which he stated:

> Under economic co-operation we must strive to spread the idea among colored people that the accumulation of wealth is for social rather than indi-

vidual ends. We must avoid, in the advancement of the Negro race the mistakes of ruthless exploitation which have marked modern economic history. To this end we must seek not simply home ownership, small landholding and saving[s] accounts, but also all forms of co-operation, both in production and distribution, profit sharing, building and loan associations, systematic charity for definite, practical ends, systematic migration from mob rule and robbery, to freedom and enfranchisement, the emancipation of women and the abolition of child labor. . . .

For the accomplishment of all these ends we must organize . . . I thank God that most of the money that supports the National Association for the Advancement of Colored People comes from black hands; a still larger proportion must so come, and we must not only support but control this and similar organizations and hold them unwaveringly to our aims and our ideals.

Dr. Du Bois' 1915 program for a planned black economy and black control over civil rights groups was more progressive than the protest, integrationist aims of the NAACP in 1920. As time passed, changes in the Doctor's thinking would ever widen the distance between his goals and those of the Association. Already in 1920 the NAACP was criticized for being too conservative. But its program was necessarily limited by the white reaction to black progress which had set in after World War I. It had been stopped in its own forward development by this postwar rise of conservatism.

The Association, therefore, was compelled to fight the terrorism of the Ku Klux Klan. It publicized the horror of lynchings and defended blacks in the courtrooms of America.

The NAACP felt that Dr. Du Bois had perhaps gone too fast when he had continued his Pan-African Congresses. The Association's fight was for blacks in America, and it would have preferred the Doctor to concentrate his considerable energies on that cause. But for Dr. Du Bois, the problems of black poverty and equality were simply parts of a larger, more profound problem. And it was the Russian Revolution of 1917 which helped to clarify his thinking about socialism and Pan-Africanism. Russia, he felt, had come forward with an answer. In an age of abundant resources and scientific technique, little had been done to ease the starvation and poverty of millions of the world's people. Russia alone believed she had the ability to feed, clothe, and provide shelter for all her people, and train them at the same time:

> Russia was trying to accomplish this by eventually putting into the hands of those people who do the world's work the power to guide and rule the state for the best welfare of the masses. It made the assumption, long disputed, that out of the downtrodden mass of people, ability and character sufficient to do this task effectively could and would be found. I believed this dictum passionately. It was, in fact, the foundation stone of my fight for black folk; it explained me.[2]

With the coming of the Russian Revolution Dr. Du Bois had begun his serious study of Karl Marx; however, he never jumped to the conclusion that the revolution had fulfilled all of Marx's predictions. Furthermore, he did not believe that the government of the United States had to be overthrown in order to achieve economic equality. He hated violence and believed that it rarely brought advancement to the world. Russian communism was not the program or the answer for American blacks, but some form of socialism surely was. He believed that there would have to be a slow, reasoned development in the production and distribution of goods in America—in short, the socialization of industry and a more equitable system of distribution.

For example, the Doctor said, the telephone company in the North employed no blacks: no clerks, no officials, and no laborers. And yet blacks who owned telephones were taxed, as were other citizens for this public service. The only solution to such blatant exclusion, he said, was government ownership of the company.

In 1920, two years after the end of the war, Dr. Du Bois was fifty-two years old. He had edited *The Crisis* continuously since its inception, and in January 1920 he began publishing another periodical, *The Brownies' Book,* "a monthly magazine for the children of the sun." Jessie Redmond Fauset, a teacher in the New York City schools and a published novelist, acted as feature editor, gathering poems, stories, and simple biographies for the children to read. She and Dr. Du Bois were quick to encourage budding writers to contribute to *The Brownies' Book;* the Doctor's own daughter, Yolande, often wrote for it.

Dr. Du Bois revealed himself through the pages of *The Brownies' Book* as "The Crow" in a column called "As the Crow Flies":

> The crow is black and O so beautiful, shining with dark blues and purples, with little hints of gold in his mighty wings. He flies far above the Earth, looking downward with his sharp eyes. What a lot of things he must see and hear and if he could only talk—and lo, *The Brownies' Book* has made him talk for you.[3]

The Crow always said how beautiful it was to be black; "I like my black feathers—don't you?"

Through *The Brownies' Book* Dr. Du Bois and his associates presented the world to boys and girls. They told the children about the black American soldier who had fought so well in the "Great War." There were stories, legends, fables, and poems from around the world. And above all, *The Brownies' Book* gave to black children a magazine published and written by the leading members of their own race. It was a magnificent achievement. Although it ceased publication in 1921, there has been nothing like it since.

In 1920 there appeared a collection of essays and poems by Dr. Du Bois called *Darkwater: Voices from Within the Veil. Darkwater* created something of a furor, for in one essay entitled "The Souls of White Folk" the Doctor stated that World War I was nothing compared to "that fight for freedom which black and brown and yellow men must and will make unless their oppression and humiliation and insult at the hands of the White World cease."

Various publications reported that Dr. Du Bois, a "mixed-blood," was leading his people "to annihilation."[4]

Such statements must have seemed amusing to the Doctor, for whatever leadership he exercised was only in the area of ideas. He was not personally popular and never paraded his family before the public in the manner of a smart politician. Aloof and scholarly, he kept his private life to himself, although it was an extremely satisfying life. By 1920 he had been married for twenty-two years to Nina Gomer Du Bois. Their only son, Burghardt, had died in infancy. Their daughter, Yolande, was a grown woman. The Doctor was a loving father and husband who doted on his family. His wife's work was in the home, and it kept her totally involved. His work was out in the world; for twenty years, into the 1930s, it was mainly responsible for changing black people's attitudes toward their condition in American society. His *Crisis* editorials, his other writings, and his speeches made black people aware of the grave and just reasons they had for discontent.

For some time, and perhaps because of the pervading racial hatred in the nation, a marvelous new spirit had been developing among black people. From their ranks in the 1920s came forth a new harvest of writers who would become their spokesmen. Black writers, artists, and playwrights, educated and talented, wanted to have all of the power and the glory America had to offer. But they wanted the Good Life on the basis of the truth and artistry of their work. They were called the New Negro; their artistic and social goals became a movement known as the Negro Renaissance. Among these writers and poets, all of whom are too numerous to list, were Countee Cullen, Jean Toomer, Langston Hughes, Arna Bontemps, and Claude McKay. James Weldon Johnson, W. E. B. Du Bois, and Alain Locke were some of the older writers whom these younger ones held in esteem.

Aaron Douglas was the leading black painter of the Negro Renaissance; his murals showed the cultural background and the warmth and vitality of black Americans. In 1927 Mr. Douglas illustrated a volume by James Weldon Johnson entitled *God's Trombones: Seven Negro Sermons in Verse* and an anthology of verse, *Caroling Dusk,* by Countee Cullen. His excellent work graced the pages of *Plays of Negro Life* by Alain Locke and *Not Without Laughter* by Langston Hughes.

Alain Locke was a distinguished professor of philosophy at Howard University in Washington, D.C. A fine critic of the arts, he was most helpful to young black artists in their never-ending search for work, sponsors, and publishers who might bring their talent to the attention of the world. Dr. Locke's anthology, *The New Negro,* published in 1925, contained essays, stories, parts of novels, and poems dealing with all areas of black life in America. Throughout this work it was clear that black writers would no longer allow themselves to be thought of as inferior. For in all of the writing there was a new feeling of power and strength, and an honest effort was made to portray black people as they were and as they lived.

The New Negro read like a *Who's Who* of the Negro Renaissance. Aaron Douglas had illustrated it with decorative designs and drawings. Walter White, who had become assistant executive secretary of the NAACP in 1918, contributed an essay entitled "The Paradox of Color." In it he told about his work reporting on lynchings for the Association. Because of his nearly white complexion, he could attend the gatherings of the Ku Klux Klan and never be recognized as a black man.

Countee Cullen, Langston Hughes, Jesse Fauset, Jean Toomer, James Weldon Johnson, and Dr. Du Bois all contributed to *The New Negro.*

In his autobiography, *The Big Sea,* Langston Hughes has described the Negro Renaissance as the time when "the Negro was in vogue." White people came to Harlem every night to mix with the black folks in the cabarets and nightclubs. Jazz swept the country; black artists flourished. The Charleston, the Black Bottom, and the Lindy Hop dances grew up in the streets of Harlem and matured in the Savoy Ballroom on Lenox

Avenue. The list of black writers, playwrights, artists, and actors was endless, as was the flow of people through the streets of Harlem.

Like Alain Locke, W. E. B. Du Bois was active in the movement to arrange for young artists new to Harlem, and sometimes lost and lonely in New York, to meet one another. He also helped by providing contacts with white authors, publishers, and potential sponsors. In 1924 he published two books, *The Gift of Black Folk* and *Dark Princess*. And his editing of *The Crisis* magazine continued; many of the new writers of the Negro Renaissance were published for the first time in its pages. There was hardly a magazine in 1924 that would go to press without printing a Countee Cullen poem. In 1928, Mr. Cullen married Dr. Du Bois' only child, Yolande, in an elaborate marriage ceremony at the Salem Methodist Episcopal Church in Harlem. Dr. Du Bois had planned and arranged the ceremony himself and Countee Cullen's father, who was pastor of the church, presided over the wedding. Among the ten ushers were Langston Hughes and Arna Bontemps. As the wedding music began and 3,000 people watched, live canaries in gilded cages sang and trilled.

The marriage did not succeed. Countee Cullen went off on a fellowship to Europe and Yolande worked as a camp counselor on Bear Mountain. They were divorced in 1930.

The Negro Renaissance flourished, and in his keynote address on the twentieth anniversary of the

NAACP in June 1929, Dr. Du Bois reflected this new spirit of black solidarity. Just twenty years before, he said, there had been hardly a scientist who "dared to assert the equality of the Negro race." Africa, it was assumed, had no history; there was but one college in all of the United States that offered a course of study in black history and psychology. From the early days of slavery, the fate of the blacks had always been thought to be death by disease, crime, and inefficiency. No one had ever expected the black African to survive for long in North America. Black people themselves had come to believe that equal rights would never be theirs.

The NAACP had disregarded this kind of thinking, the Doctor went on to say. It had agitated, protested, and pushed its way into the courts. It had demanded the right to vote and had urged black children into college: "We studied African history and in season and out of season we declared that the colored races were destined at least to share in the heritage of the earth."

So Dr. W. E. B. Du Bois spoke at a period when it seemed that the great times of the 1920s would never end. His strategy had not changed much over the years. The difference now was that more black people were ready and willing to stand with him for a more aggressive policy. They were ever more eager to transform their rising race pride into social action.

But the Great Depression lay just ahead. The Negro Renaissance, although vital to the development of black artists, hardly touched the lives of the poor black masses. The circulation of *The Crisis* had begun to shrink. Clashes between Dr. Du Bois and Walter White of the NAACP were becoming serious. Many called the Doctor "the old Du Bois." They believed him to be out of place with the image of the "New Negro," and they felt that black progress was best served by continuing with more determination the program of legal protest and integration of the past.

For the most part, the "New Negro" ignored Dr. Du Bois' program for a planned black economy. The Doctor was sixty-one years old, an age when many men would have thought seriously about ending public life. The young, vigorous years of work and struggle had passed with incredible swiftness. But Dr. Du Bois would live more than thirty years longer. Fine deeds and dreadful ordeals, also, awaited him.

CHAPTER 11

The BLACK RENAIS-
sance of the 1920s had brought some financial security
to the small middle class of blacks in the United States.
In the country as a whole there was a sense of prosperity never known before. A team of economists in 1929
was amazed at the "outpouring of energy" which in just
seven years had piled up skyscrapers in scores of cities;
knit the forty-eight states together with 20,000 miles
of airways; moved more than a billion and a half tons
of freight over railroads and waterways; thronged the
highways with 25 million motor cars; carried electricity
to 17 million homes, and fed, clothed, housed, and
amused the 120 million persons who occupy our twentieth of the habitable area of the earth.

The facts suggested a false prosperity, for Good
Times did not touch such important economic areas as
agriculture, shipbuilding, the railway-equipment business, or the coal, textile, and shoe industries. Even so,
the ordinary man in the street "became dizzy with ex-

pectation." Millions of people found themselves caught up in installment buying, a method which permitted them to purchase goods and make fixed payments for them at intervals over a long period of time.

In 1928 and 1929, values on the stock market went up out of proportion to the stocks' present or expected future earnings. Brokerage houses did not take the time to give their customers honest, cautious advice. Stockbrokers became high-pressure salesmen who cared little about the worth of what they were selling. People took the savings of a lifetime out of banks, or mortgaged their homes to buy stocks, hoping to double—even triple—their money on the stock market. The Federal Reserve Board restricted bank credit, hoping but failing to stop stock speculation. And in late October 1929 good stocks along with risky, inflated stocks fell in price on the stock market. The Great Depression had begun.

Blinded by visions of sudden wealth, America had been unable to see that the national prosperity was not spread evenly among all levels of society. The new technology with its labor-saving methods had thrown two million men out of work in the seven years before 1928. The methods of many new businesses were reckless and often corrupt. State and municipal governments piled up mountainous debts. Political and economic unrest in foreign countries endangered American investments abroad. America's tariff rate for incoming foreign goods was rising, which caused other countries to retaliate by raising their own tarifs. This economic crisis became the worst America had ever known. In human terms, it spread ruin through every part of the country and every level of the population. Prices fell; business shrank; factories and mines shut down. By 1930 some five million men had been thrown out of work. A severe, prolonged drought in the summer brought even more suffering, for crops in thirty states were nearly worthless.

The black renaissance ended with the crash which brought everything else down like a house of cards. More than half of the black population was unemployed. Everywhere there were breadlines and soup kitchens for starving people. Thousands were evicted from their homes for nonpayment of rent or mortgages. They set up tar-paper and tin shanty towns on the outskirts of the cities. A million people out of work rode freight trains, hitched rides on the highways, or walked across the country hunting work. They died by the hundreds of starvation, disease, and exposure to severe cold or heat. Indescribable suffering was everywhere. It was shocking, and nowhere could there be seen an end to it.

The Crisis magazine, like so many others, was no longer able to stand independently. Its circulation had shrunk drastically with the coming of the Depression. If it were to survive, Dr. Du Bois knew he must have help from the main office of the NAACP. But if the NAACP supported *The Crisis,* it would have the right to tell the Doctor what he could print.

While *The Crisis* was having financial troubles, Dr. Du Bois came into conflict with the Association. With people actually starving, he wanted the NAACP to pay more attention to the black masses in terms of money and food for them. The Doctor pressed for organized economic cooperation among blacks. The Republican Herbert Hoover had been elected President of the United States in 1928 when it seemed that Good Times might last forever. Blacks had traditionally supported the party of Abraham Lincoln. But now they identified the Republican party, and Herbert Hoover, with the Depression.

In 1932 there were 14 million people unemployed, and there was widespread hunger and despair among blacks. President Hoover, reflecting the optimism of a confident capitalist system, felt that involvement of the federal government in the economy was wrong. He was certain that the business cycle which had brought on the Depression would bring about prosperity again. Finally, his administration did have to act. It gave assistance to banks and railroads. It expanded credit and helped save some farmers and homeowners from complete ruin. But the president remained steadfastly against direct government relief to the jobless. So it was that business failures, unemployment, farm failures, and hunger continued.

In the 1932 presidential election the lower middle classes of the cities, the millions of unemployed workers and long-suffering farmers elected the first Democratic president since Woodrow Wilson. The man was Franklin Delano Roosevelt, and he initiated reform legislation that was a combination of national recovery and relief. This social legislation was known as the New Deal.

The 1930s turned out to be something of a nightmare for the whole world. Each nation tried to separate its economy from the economy of every other nation; each tried to live within itself, for the demand of people everywhere was for security. In countries that were strongly democratic this need gave rise to economic reform and public welfare programs. Thus the New Deal helped to protect the American worker from long-term unemployment and future disasters.

But many believed that democracy was suited only to wealthy countries. It was unfortunately true that totalitarianism spread at an alarming rate during this period of crisis. Everywhere unemployed people cried out for a leader who would act quickly and get results. This feeling was partly responsible for President Roosevelt's popularity and the strong public response to his reform programs. In other countries it opened the way for absolute dictators to take control. In Germany the wealthy barons from the mining and industrial center of the Ruhr River valley took advantage of the economic confusion. Their financial power and Germany's mounting political chaos made it possible for Adolf Hitler to become chancellor in 1933 without ever having won an election.

Hitler believed in a German "master race" of people

he called Aryans, an ancient word whose meaning he distorted to signify a Caucasian who had no Jewish ancestry. His solution to Germany's economic and political problems was war, and his "final solution" to what he believed to be the Jewish problem was the systematic extermination of millions of Jews.

In the United States, with the coming of the New Deal, black Americans received some attention from a hard-pressed government. The question facing Dr. Du Bois was what could be done in the future to bring about a planned black economy. The development of such an economy within the established capitalist system would present the problem of deliberate racial segregation. Furthermore, black and white liberals within the NAACP, who had fought for black equality on every level, would be against any race separation.

Walter White had become executive secretary of the Association in 1931, when James Weldon Johnson resigned from the post. Three years later Dr. Du Bois wrote in *The Crisis* that the NAACP had been founded at a period when the masses of black children were being trained in black schools and black churchgoers were worshipping in black churches. At that time, he said, a slogan of "no segregation" would have been impossible. The Association was an organization that never had taken, and never could take, an absolute stand against race segregation.

Perhaps seeing the Du Bois statement as a criticism of the very basis for the NAACP, Walter White stated in *The Crisis* of March 1934, "The historic position of the NAACP has from the date of its foundation been opposed to segregation."

After both Dr. Du Bois and Mr. White had made their positions clear, the NAACP Board of Directors voted that "no salaried officer of the Association shall criticize the policy, work, or officers of the Association in the pages of *The Crisis*."

Dr. Du Bois had advocated a planned black economy because he was deeply concerned about finding more jobs and more income for the hard-pressed mass of black people. It was his belief that the NAACP had always supported black institutions and now was confusing segregation with discrimination. He genuinely felt that black separatism was not always wrong. And since race hatred in America was overwhelmingly powerful, he saw no solution for blacks unless they developed their own resources. Once black people had developed a "closed economic circle" of their own, they could then more sensibly turn their attention to integration.

After the NAACP voted that the Association could not be criticized in *The Crisis,* Dr. Du Bois felt he could no longer stay on as editor. He handed in his resignation, which the board finally accepted. The NAACP wrote kindly in appreciation of the fine work he had done over the years: "He created, what never existed before, a Negro intelligentsia, and many who have never read a word of his writings are his spiritual disciples and descendants. Without him the Association would never have been what it was and is."

In 1934, at the age of sixty-six, Dr. Du Bois found himself cut off from what had been his life. He had conceived of *The Crisis* and had made it his powerful voice. Now he must hand it over to others. The hurt, the pain of it went deep, and leaving the Association meant leaving friends of twenty-five years. But leave he did.

John Hope, former president of Morehouse University and lifelong friend of Dr. Du Bois, was now president of Atlanta University. He had for many years been asking the Doctor to return to Atlanta. The Doctor wrote that John Hope promised him "leisure for thought and writing, and freedom of expression, so far, of course, as Georgia would permit it."

Thus in 1934 Dr. Du Bois resumed his duties in the Department of Sociology at Atlanta University as an elder statesman. No longer the center of controversy, he still was a man of great intelligence and prestige. He lectured at leading universities throughout the North and received honorary degrees from Fisk University, Wilberforce University, and Atlanta University.

At Atlanta he sought to begin again his former program of research on the black American. He founded the magazine *Phylon,* which was to be a review of "Race and Culture." The Carnegie Foundation granted him financial aid to sponsor the first Phylon Institute. And in 1940 he asked black colleges to help in a study of the status of the so-called Negro race.

During the years of his return to Atlanta Dr. Du

Bois wrote two major works. One was entitled *Black Reconstruction in America: 1860–1880*. In this work he attempted to show how the theories of Karl Marx related to the period of Reconstruction after the Civil War. More significant was the fact that *Black Reconstruction* revealed for the first time the extraordinary contribution of blacks to southern government during the period of Reconstruction. Previously Reconstruction had been shown as a chaotic time. Southern blacks had been portrayed as dishonest, ignorant, and often more dangerous than the bigoted southern whites. *Black Reconstruction* remains today one of the finest statements of black activity in southern government after the Civil War.

Several years later, at the age of seventy-two, Dr. Du Bois published *Dusk of Dawn,* subtitled *An Essay Toward an Autobiography of a Race Concept*. In this volume he revealed his role, step by step, in the black man's fight for freedom in America and Africa: "My life had its significance and its only deep significance because it was part of a Problem; but that problem was, as I continue to think, the central problem of the greatest of the world's democracies and so the Problem of the future world." Throughout this book the Doctor traced his own changing concepts in the face of black-white conflicts; his life, he felt, was a case study of ever-maturing ideas. *Dusk of Dawn* is one of Dr. Du Bois' most appealing books—an unforgettable record of his changing life and the times through which he lived.

Phylon, the quarterly magazine that Dr. Du Bois began publishing at Atlanta University in 1940, continued under his direction for four years. It is still being published today. In its pages in 1940 the Doctor asked for the reestablishment of his earlier study of black problems. The story of the black American living at the time of the Depression had never been told. More than a third of the blacks in the cities had been placed on public charity. Many more probably needed help but were discriminated against. The greater tragedy, as Dr. Du Bois saw it, was "the loss of thousands of farms and homes, the disappearance of savings among the rising Negro middle class, the collapse of Negro banks, insurance companies and retail business." For from the middle class came what limited leadership the black race had.

Dr. Du Bois and John Hope planned to build at Atlanta University the best institution of higher learning that the state of Georgia had ever known. But the university did not have enough money to support the Doctor's program for scientific investigation and publication. He found it necessary to go to black schools "from Virginia to Texas in order to see what cooperation I could start."

Meanwhile, World War II had begun with an assault on Poland. Over a million men of the German armed forces, with armored divisions and the air power of the Luftwaffe, subdued the ill-equipped Polish armies. Germans suddenly overran Norway, Denmark, and the

Netherlands in April and May of 1940. Taking the French and British by surprise, German divisions drove deep into northern France. And British forces and some French divisions had to retreat to the beaches of Dunkirk on the North Sea.

By June 22 France sued for peace, and an armistice was signed. And with the fall of France, Germany stood ready to invade Britain. But Adolf Hitler had not expected such thorough success in Europe and had no firm battle plan ready for the invasion. It was for this reason that the Battle of Britain went on for months, taking the form of an air offensive. The Germans were unable to overcome the British Royal Air Force, however, which gradually fought off the German Luftwaffe with greater success. Most importantly, life in Britain carried on even though the industry of the country was seriously disrupted and thousands of people killed.

Dr. Du Bois wrote in 1941, "If Hitler wins, every single right we now possess, for which we have struggled here in America for more than three centuries, will be instantaneously wiped out."

The Japanese in 1941 had been conducting a war against China for ten years. As all of Europe went to war, the Japanese saw the time as perfect for them to assert themselves throughout the Far East. Japan had bound itself in a three-power pact with Germany and Italy in 1940. In 1941 it had signed a neutrality treaty with Russia. The Japanese prime minister, General Hideki Tojo, stated publicly that all United States and

British influence in the Orient would be eliminated, but he did agree to send representatives to Washington for negotiations. As these negotiations were taking place, the Japanese attacked the American naval base at Pearl Harbor in Hawaii. The air raid came without warning on December 7, 1941, with attacks at the same time on Guam and Midway islands and on Hong Kong and Malaya. The United States and Britain declared war on Japan on December 8. Germany and Italy declared war on the United States three days later.

A year later, in 1942, the United States was still mobilizing and converting industry to the production of war materials for itself and its allies. The government imposed controls on the economy to prevent inflation; it set up a compulsory military draft and a system of civil defense. More than a million black Americans, both men and women, entered the armed forces. However, as late as 1940 in New York City only a hundred or so blacks were among 30,000 workers in defense plants. Again and again black leaders asked President Roosevelt to open defense jobs to everyone. Then A. Philip Randolph, editor of the *Messenger* and founder of the Brotherhood of Sleeping Car Porters, announced that he was planning a protest march on Washington. The march was to be a "nonviolent demonstration of Negro mass power."

For the first time, black Americans were able to pressure the government into changing national policy. On June 25, 1941, President Roosevelt issued Executive Order #8802 banning discrimination in all plants working on national defense contracts. This order established the Committee on Fair Employment Practices within the Office of Production Management. But the order was limited to vocational-training programs and employment only in defense industries. The president declined to issue a broader order which might have barred discrimination in military services as black spokesmen had wished. Black soldiers were still segregated in separate units.

As had happened in the past, during the Civil War and World War I, the United States recognized the necessity for reform and justice when it needed the help of black Americans. But always uncertain was how much racial justice would be granted to blacks, and how fast what little was given would be allowed to come.

At this time Dr. Du Bois was able to interest the presidents of southern black land-grant colleges in his program for black studies. The land-grant colleges had been established by the Morrill Act in 1862, which allowed each state loyal to the Union 30,000 acres for the purpose of endowing at least one agricultural college.

The federal government in 1935 gave $18 million a year to land-grant colleges in southern states. Blacks, who formed over 20 percent of the southern population, received only about 5 percent of this money. Black colleges had been pressing for a larger share but were told that such work as research in agriculture or chemistry was being done in white colleges, that there was no need for duplicating such programs in black colleges. Dr. Du Bois felt that a program of black studies in the black colleges was an honest demand for a greater share of federal funds, and he presented his program to the land-grant-college presidents. In June 1942 they adopted his general plan, which in part, proposed to "initiate a series of cooperative studies of the social condition of the American Negro and more especially of his economic situation during and after this war."

Dr. Du Bois was designated the official coordinator of the proposed sociological studies to be instituted by the land-grant colleges. A second meeting of college presidents was planned for the spring of 1944. The Doctor wrote in July 1943 concerning the conditions black Americans would face after the war:

There is going to be increased race friction and finally want and unemployment in the midst of violent social change. At such time we want accurate and carefully made social measurements, tested techniques and the machinery for further investigation. There will be neither time nor disposition during times of turmoil to initiate new and calm investigation. If now we begin this nationwide study of economic and social conditions, it can be continuously pursued through storm and stress and after the post-war calm and form a priceless guide to social survival and lasting peace.[1]

The Doctor's prophetic words would prove to be, unfortunately, true. Most black World War II veterans would come home to find few jobs open to them and not enough homes to go around. They would face renewed discrimination, which they had been told they had been fighting to destroy in Europe and Asia.

Then, just when Dr. Du Bois' careful plan for broad study of his people seemed so successful, came, as he put it, "catastrophe."

Without notice, he was retired from the Department of Sociology at Atlanta University. The reason remains unclear and has not yet been discussed publicly. In any case, the result was that the Doctor found himself at the age of seventy-six without a job and with less than $5,000 in savings. His great plan for scientific study was destroyed in its beginning.

The presidents of land-grant colleges had been willing to work with Dr. Du Bois because of his experience, his scholarship, and his many significant published works. In short, they trusted his judgment and his extraordinary intelligence. Without him the program for black studies died in two years. It was never revived on so broad a scale. And only recently have limited black studies programs been proposed.

"I felt the world tottering beneath my feet and I fought back in despair. . . . It was not my youth that I was losing; it was my old age; and old age was worthless in the United States."

CHAPTER 12

IN 1944 THE NAACP urged Dr. Du Bois to return to the organization. Walter White, remembering his past contributions, was very much in favor of this. So it happened that the Doctor willingly rejoined the Association to revive the pan-African movement and to "give general attention to the foreign aspects of the race problem." It was made clear to him that he would stay with the Association for the rest of his public life. However, it soon became apparent that Dr. Du Bois and the NAACP leaders had totally different ideas as to what he was to do.

Since the Doctor was seventy-five, many assumed that his life work was done. He would want comfort, they felt, a place to rest with one eye on his black people and one on his dreams. For this reason some in the organization thought the Doctor would, as he said, "Willingly act as window dressing, say a proper word now and then and give the Association and its Secretary moral support. This theory did not occur to me. I had no thought of doing nothing or of subordinating myself entirely to anybody in thought or deed."

Dr. Du Bois understood that he was to give advice when it was asked of him; revive the Pan-African Congresses, and cooperate with everyone without being subordinate to anyone in the organization. He served as an associate consultant to the American delegation of the United Nations founding conference in San Francisco in 1945. When he later returned to New York, he charged that the UN's charter prevented it from intervening in the administration of colonies. This meant to the Doctor that countries in Africa and Asia administered by foreign governments were not protected by the UN. Dr. Du Bois then announced a meeting of the Sixth Pan-African Congress,[1] which, like those that had taken place twenty-five years before, would bring pressure on powerful countries to give home rule to their colonies.

The congress met in England in the fall of 1945 under the leadership of George Padmore, secretary of the newly formed Pan-African Federation and originally from Trinidad. Kwame Nkrumah of Ghana, Africa, was elected political secretary, and Jomo Kenyatta of Kenya was assistant secretary. Dr. Du Bois was elected International President of the Pan-African Congress.

As he had in Atlanta, the Doctor settled back again into the role of elder statesman. He was called the "Father" of pan-Africanism by George Padmore and warmly regarded as the "Grand Old Man of pan-Africanism" by the young African and West Indian leaders. They knew of his earlier congresses beginning in 1918; the Doctor could not have been more pleased by their obvious affection for him. His earlier congresses and his crusade for a free Africa had been thwarted by white reaction to black progress after World War I and by the Garvey Movement, which appealed directly to the hurt and suffering of oppressed black Americans. Perhaps now, the Doctor felt, the American black race had advanced far enough to concern itself with the fate of the mother continent.

The Sixth Pan-African Congress of 1945 brought together intellectuals, civic leaders, workers, farmers, and students. In its Declaration to the Colonial Workers, Farmers, and Intellectuals the congress stated: "We affirm the right of all Colonial People to control their own destiny. All colonies must be free from foreign imperialist control, whether political or economic."[2]

This was the embodiment of pan-Africanism. With "Africa for the Africans" as its call to action, a free Africa could unite with oppressed peoples everywhere who wished to throw off the mantle of colonialism.

While at the NAACP, Dr. Du Bois continued his astonishingly wide range of pursuits. He wrote articles, pamphlets, and newspaper columns. He attended conferences and "travelled 20,000 miles to deliver 150 lectures on subjects connected with my work for the

NAACP as I conceive it." He was instructor for two semesters at the New School for Social Research in New York; he was guest speaker at Vassar, Yale, and Princeton. He wrote two books on colonies and Africa —*Color and Democracy* in 1945 and *The World and Africa* in 1947.

But by far the most significant contribution the Doctor made at this time was a petition to the United Nations, "An Appeal to the World" which was instigated as a direct result of the Sixth Pan-African Congress. The appeal was presented to the UN in the form of six essays by separate authors. One, written by the Doctor, stated in part:

> A discrimination practiced in the United States against her own citizens and to a large extent in contravention of her own laws, cannot be persisted in without infringing upon the rights of the peoples of the world and especially upon the ideals and the work of the United Nations . . . it is, therefore, fitting and proper that the 13 million American citizens of Negro descent should appeal to the United Nations and ask that organization in the proper way to take cognizance of a situation which deprives this group of their rights as men and citizens, and by so doing makes the functioning of the United Nations more difficult, if not in many cases impossible.[3]

The Soviet Union believed that the "Appeal" should have a hearing, but the United States opposed it successfully. From this time onward, Dr. Du Bois increasingly supported programs and groups promoting peace and friendship with the Soviet Union. Looking at the international scene in the years after World War II, the Doctor believed the Soviet Union to be the only world power which practiced racial equality and stood openly against colonialism.

In 1948 Dr. Du Bois made speeches for the newly formed Progressive party, seeking to win votes for Henry Wallace, who was the party's choice for president. Wallace was outspoken on equal rights for blacks, and in favor of peace and friendship with the Soviet Union.

In September of the same year Walter White was made consultant to the American delegation to the United Nations General Assembly in Paris. Dr. Du Bois criticized White's acceptance of the post, saying that it appeared to bind the NAACP to support Democrat Harry S. Truman in his bid for election. This opinion was expressed in a private memorandum, which somehow the newspapers got hold of soon after it was written. Although the Doctor informed the NAACP board that he had not released this memorandum to the public he was dismissed from his position with the Association.

For the second time Dr. Du Bois' work with the NAACP ended, and for the second time in four years he found himself abruptly without a job. Controversy, confrontation, seemed to follow him wherever he went.

The reasons for this were abundantly clear. What Dr. Du Bois believed to be true he stated in no uncertain terms and let the chips fall where they might. Logical and honest almost to a fault, and perhaps more than a bit arrogant, he often found himself embroiled in bitter public disputes before he knew it. It may have been for the best that this second break with the NAACP occurred when it did. Years before, he had gone beyond protest and beyond black nationalism to the far side of pan-Africanism. Beginning from the narrow view of one special group of blacks, Dr. Du Bois had come to what he believed was the heart of the matter —a world view of freedom for all men who labor.

Significantly, in 1947, the United States had instituted far-reaching foreign policy changes. Under the Truman Doctrine the United States pledged itself to the containment of communism and the Soviet Union. America would aid Greece and Turkey, who were both thought by America to be threatened with communist takeover by the Soviets, and would halt anywhere in Europe aggression by subversion or attack.

The same year, the Marshall Plan was launched, the purpose of which was to revive "a working economy in the world so as to permit the emergence of political and social conditions in which free institutions can exist." The United States would give financial aid to help revive the postwar economies of European nations. Soviet Foreign Minister Vyacheslav Molotov claimed that the Marshall Plan was no better than an "imperialist" plot to enslave the whole of Europe, to make Europe dependent on the United States.

So began the "Cold War," in which the United States and the Soviet Union became entrenched in an incriminating relationship. They were the only two great powers still standing strong after World War II. With their vastly different economic systems and governments, they felt compelled to distrust one another. When one took measures for its own security, the other felt it an act of provocation. Smaller countries found themselves in sympathy with one side or the other. Relentlessly the world was becoming two armed camps with the Soviet Union and the United States as cold, calculating enemies. In America any group expressing sympathy for the Soviets had a difficult time indeed.

The United States in 1948, therefore, was not a particularly healthy place for a man with liberal, leftist ideas such as Dr. Du Bois held. Immediately after his dismissal from the NAACP, he was offered and accepted the honorary position of vice-chairman of the Council on African Affairs. The Council was an organization of American blacks who wished in some way to pay homage and give service to Africa. The Doctor took the position because of his faith in all things African and because of his deep regard for Paul Robeson, who had helped to establish the Council in New York. But soon the Council on African Affairs was declared "subversive" and placed on the U.S. attorney general's list of organizations allegedly sympathetic to communism. The Council's work was thus hampered, and its membership fell away.

In March 1949 Dr. Du Bois, with his great concern for bringing permanent peace to the world, was a sponsor of the Conference on Peace which took place at the Waldorf Astoria Hotel in New York. O. John Rogge, former U.S. assistant attorney general and known as a liberal lawyer, wrote the Doctor of the need for such a meeting to bring together representatives of the nations of the world. As a sponsor, Dr. Du Bois spoke at the last meeting of the Conference held in Madison Square Garden:

> . . . we are not traitors nor conspirators; and far from plotting force and violence, it is precisely force and violence that we bitterly oppose. This Conference was not called to defend communism nor socialism nor the American way of life. It was called to promote peace. . . . [4]

In April of the same year, at Mr. Rogge's invitation, Dr. Du Bois attended the World Peace Congress held in Paris, where he said:

> . . . Socialism is spreading all over the world and even in the United States. . . . Against this spread of socialism, one modern institution is working desperately and this is colonialism, and colonialism has been and is and ever will be one of the chief causes of war. . . . Drunk with power we are leading the world to hell in a new colonialism with the same old human

slavery which once ruined us; and to a Third World War which will ruin the world.[5]

In March 1950 Dr. Du Bois became an official of the Peace Information Center. Its object was to make the American public aware of the work other nations were undertaking to promote peace. Among other things the Center reprinted and circulated the Stockholm Peace Appeal to abolish the atomic bomb, collecting two and a half million signatures in support of it. Unanimously adopted at a meeting of the World Partisans of Peace in Stockholm March 15, 1950, the appeal read:

> We demand the absolute banning of the atomic weapon, an arm of terror and of mass extermination of populations.
> We demand the establishment of strict international control to ensure the implementation of this ban.
> We consider that the first government henceforth to use the atomic weapon against any country whatsoever will be committing a crime against humanity and should be treated as a war criminal.
> We call on all people of good will throughout the world to sign this appeal.[6]

Half a billion people signed the Stockholm Peace Appeal, but Secretary of State Dean Acheson denounced it as a "propaganda trick" of the Soviet Union.[7] Dr. Du Bois immediately replied to him in a press release, pointing out that America had to live in the world with Russia and China. If we had been able to work together with the Russians against Hitler during World War II, surely we could work with them for peace.

The Doctor traveled to Russia in the fall of 1950 to attend the All-Union Conference of Peace Proponents in Moscow. Then he attended a meeting of the Bureau of the World Congress of the Defenders of Peace in Prague, Czechoslovakia, to add demands for disarmament to the Stockholm Peace Appeal and to plan another World Peace Congress.

In Paris, on his way home from Prague, Dr. Du Bois received a message from the American Labor party asking him to run for the Senate as a candidate from New York. A second message informed the Doctor that the Department of Justice had demanded that the Peace Information Center register as "agents of a foreign principal," or power. Any organization that the Justice Department deemed sympathetic to communism, that it believed to be acting in behalf of any foreign country, Communist or non-Communist, had to register with the government under the Foreign Agents Registration Act of 1938.

Today such words as "agent of a foreign principal" have little or no meaning. But in 1950 in the United States they were cause enough for a man's friends to turn from him in fear and cease to associate with him. He might be fired from his job, and his name stricken from all public records. Even if the charge were unjust and untrue, the mere accusation could cause him to be treated as a criminal, losing his good name and the good name of his family. This was exactly what happened to the world-renowned Dr. W. E. B. Du Bois.

CHAPTER 13

$\mathbf{T}$HE U.S. GOVERNMENT
in 1947 had begun investigating the loyalty of government workers. Congress increased its pressure to hunt for communists among civil servants, and the government became more and more severe in its attitude toward individuals and groups who were "liberal" and tolerant toward our former ally, the Soviet Union.

In 1949 eleven major officials of the United States Communist party were found guilty of conspiring to advocate the overthrow of the government by violence. They were convicted under the Smith Act of 1940 and given prison sentences.

The Committee on Un-American Activities in the House of Representatives heard testimony that persons who had held office during the Franklin D. Roosevelt administration were secret supporters of the Communist party. Most liberals at first considered such stories pure fantasy. But in 1950 a former State Department official, Alger Hiss, was put on trial for perjury. He had denied charges that in 1938 he had given confidential information to Russia. Mr. Hiss had been accused by Whittaker Chambers, an admitted former courier for the Communists. When Mr. Hiss sued Mr. Chambers for libel, Mr. Chambers produced State Department documents that Mr. Hiss had supposedly given him. Mr. Hiss was convicted on November 17, 1949, and sentenced to five years in prison. The Hiss conviction helped to lend credit to the claim by extreme conservatives in the United States that the Roosevelt New Deal had been directed by Communist agents.

Senator Joseph McCarthy, Republican from Wisconsin, insisted that the Department of State was filled with hidden Communists. The public hearings he held as chairman of the Senate Subcommittee on Un-American Activities aroused a witch-hunting hysteria in the whole country. Friends of a lifetime might accuse one another of being "red" (Communist) or "pink" (Communist-sympathizers).

The subcommittee itself caused a number of innocent people to lose their jobs and reputations as a result of their "guilt by association." Support of so-called left-wing causes such as the peace movement, or a show of understanding toward Communists was reason enough for writers, actors, teachers, and other citizens to fall under suspicion. Many were forced out of their jobs—blacklisted—and were unable to work for years. This suppression of civil liberties was most alarming. It showed clearly how successfully organized reactionary groups could apply pressure to impose their opinions on every citizen.

Dr. Du Bois, on his way home from Prague in 1950, did not take too seriously the government's request that the Peace Information Center register as a foreign agent. He was certain that the request was a mistake, or at most an attempt to slow down the organization's activities for peace. He suggested that an attorney be sent to Washington until he could go himself.

Then the Doctor forgot the whole thing and turned his attention to what he felt was a much more serious concern—his lack of experience in politics and his reluctance to run for the Senate at his age. In 1950 the Doctor was eighty-two years old. He had been in the public eye fighting for liberal causes most of his adult life. Still in good health, he worked as hard as ever, but he needed longer periods for rest. He could not quite understand how he, with his radical reputation, could add anything to the American Labor party campaign. He was told that the campaign would give him a chance to express his ideas for peace to a wide audience. Furthermore, his candidacy would help the campaign of Vito Marcantonio, congressman from New York, who hoped to be reelected.

Dr. Du Bois had supported the Progressive party campaign in 1948. He had been honorary chairman of the Council of African Affairs because of his strong belief in Pan-Africa and his deep regard for Paul Robeson. This and his participation in peace congresses at home and abroad caused him to be viewed increasingly as a dangerous radical. He was, after 1948, publishing only in liberal, left-wing publications. Moreover, his opportunity to publish in the black press became, as he put it, "narrower and narrower."

Making it even more difficult for peace-loving men to be heard was the outbreak of the Korean War in June 1950. President Truman urged Congress to enact a $10 billion rearmament program and asked for partial mobilization of American resources to meet the crisis in Korea. Clearly, then, the United States was at war, although Congress, which was entrusted under the Constitution with the power to declare war, had never made such a declaration against North Korea.

Finally, Dr. Du Bois decided to run for senator on the American Labor party ticket, and during his campaign he made ten speeches and seven radio broadcasts. His last speech in New York took place on October 24, 1950, in Madison Square Garden. Although an audience of 17,000 came to hear him, the New York press ignored the meeting.

Dr. Du Bois seemed to enjoy his new role of political campaigner. Although he lost the election, over 200,-000 persons voted for him.

The Justice Department continued to demand that the Peace Information Center register as a foreign agent, although the Center had written the Department that it was "American in its conception and formation," that it acted "only for itself," and was supported by no "foreign principal." Its attorney told Washington that

> The inference which you and the Department have made seems to be founded only on the fact that there are people throughout the world who may have, and be expressing ideas and concepts similar to those expressed by the Peace Information Center. . . . It would seem, therefore, to be a startlingly new pattern of reasoning that any idea or activity which is not . . . confined to the United States, will subject its holder to the inference that he acts for some person abroad.[1]

Then, on February 9, 1951, the Center received word that a grand jury in Washington had indicted the organization and its officers for "failure to register as agents of a foreign principal."

Dr. Du Bois, with the other officials of the Peace Information Center, and the stenographer, were indicted as criminals. And no other act affecting his life so humiliated and discouraged the Doctor. That the country which he had tried all of his life to make a more perfect place should suddenly indict him for treason was an incredible act of cruelty, to say nothing of the injustice of the charge. But like so many hundreds of others, Dr. Du Bois had become a casualty in the brooding battles of the Cold War.

The indictment was a terrible ordeal for the Doctor. He was an old man now. His wife, Nina, had died, as had many of his friends, and his New England aloofness did not make it easy for him to find new friends. However, he had years earlier met a minister's daughter whom he greatly admired. She was Shirley Graham, born in 1904 in Indianapolis. A writer with a Master of Arts degree from Oberlin College in Ohio, she was the author of plays and several biographies of blacks. Among them were *Dr. George Washington Carver, Scientist; Paul Robeson, Citizen of the World;* and a life of Frederick Douglass, *There Was Once a Slave,* which won her the Julian Messner Award.

Dr. Du Bois helped Miss Graham with her writing and took great pleasure in her literary success. She was one of his closest companions. They took out a marriage license the day the Peace Information Center indictment was handed down. The next week, the officials of the Center were to be arraigned in Washington.

Miss Graham completely understood the seriousness of the arraignment. She knew that if Dr. Du Bois went to jail, his wife would be permitted to see him. Although Dr. Du Bois and Miss Graham had planned to marry in any case, they now decided to do so as soon as possible. So it was that on February 14, 1951, a quiet ceremony took place at the home of the Reverend Edward McGowan.

Long before the Peace Information Center was indicted, the Council on African Affairs had requested that a birthday dinner be planned for Dr. Du Bois. The dinner was to take place on February 23 at the Essex House Hotel in midtown Manhattan. Dr. E. Franklin

Frazier, sociologist at Howard University and Dr. Du Bois' colleague, was chairman of the Dinner Committee. The Committee had been donated space by the African Art shop in Harlem. When news of the indictment spread, the phone kept ringing for requests for reservations to the dinner.

On Monday, the officials of the Peace Information Center were arraigned. Then Dr. Du Bois was fingerprinted, asked about his life and work, and told to remove his coat and empty his pockets. He was then searched for concealed weapons. Next he was handcuffed to another official of the Center. When one of his attorneys protested, the handcuffs were finally taken off.

Dr. Du Bois and the other officials of the Center were freed on bail, which was set at $1,000 each. The trial was not scheduled to begin for six months, and the whole period of waiting was a nightmare for the Doctor. If convicted, he could be sentenced to five years in prison and fined $10,000.

At the time of his arraignment some three hundred persons had made reservations for his birthday dinner. But on February 19 the Essex House Hotel canceled the contract for the dinner—"pursuant to our rules and regulations and for other sufficient reasons. . . ."

After this cancellation the three speakers for the dinner decided not to attend. Some sponsors withdrew, and the Doctor felt that plans for the celebration ought to be dropped. But E. Franklin Frazier insisted that the dinner must go on as scheduled. For the Doctor's friends the affair had become a fight for individual rights and the right of assembly. The Doctor was being described as a criminal by some publications, and no hotel in downtown New York City would consent to accommodate a dinner party for him.

Finally, Small's Paradise, the restaurant and night-club in Harlem, offered its facilities. Some seven hundred people attended, crowding into a space much too small, and many had to stand. E. Franklin Frazier, Paul Robeson, and Dr. Du Bois all spoke to the guests.

So it was that the Birthday Dinner for Dr. Du Bois was held in public. It may not have been the happiest of times, but it was a festive party. The people who attended were warm in their praise for the distinguished old man who needed them.

CHAPTER 14

PEOPLE ALL OVER THE world were shocked and horrified when they saw newspaper photographs of W. E. B. Du Bois handcuffed following his arraignment in Washington, D.C. Black people felt that this manacling—indeed, the whole matter of the indictment—was just another example of the constant pressure being used to frighten black leaders into silence. The State Department continued to insist that it had "irrefutable proof" that the funds of the Peace Information Center "came from Moscow."

The Center's lawyers laid down the legal foundation for the defense of the Doctor and the other officials. But a court case of this kind needed a law firm with a national reputation to gain publicity for the clients. Dr. Du Bois wrote to at least six leading lawyers, only to have all of them decline, including Arthur Garfield Hays of the American Civil Liberties Union. Then Vito Marcantonio, the former congressman of the East Harlem, New York, district, offered his services free of charge. He was made chief counsel for the defense.

Many of the Doctor's friends felt that securing Mr. Marcantonio was a mistake and would cause the defense to be associated with "subversive" elements. But the officials of the Center believed that they had made the right choice.

Dr. Du Bois never dreamed how costly justice could be in the United States, but he fully expected to take the case on up to the Supreme Court if necessary, in order to test the constitutionality of the Foreign Agents Act. When he learned that such a court case would cost at least $100,000, he was discouraged for weeks.

Dr. Du Bois appealed to the people of the United States and of the world for help. Protests to the U.S. government came quickly from individuals and countries throughout the world when they learned that the Doctor was threatened with jail. Perhaps the most stunning protest came from the International Union of Students, for it reveals that even in 1951 students were, as they are today, in the forefront of the world peace movement:

> On behalf of over 5,000,000 students in 71 countries, the International Union of Students expresses indignation at the prosecution of Dr. Du Bois and associates. Du Bois (is an) internationally known scholar and spokesman for peace. (His) work for peace is in the best traditions of the American Negro people.

Prosecution is an attack upon peace supporters, upon Negro people and upon [the] right of professors and students to act for peace. We join with peace-loving people throughout the world in demanding that you dismiss Du Bois' indictment and end persecution of United States peace supporters.[1]

Dr. Du Bois and his wife made two trips across the country to bring his case before the American people and to raise funds for his trial. They spoke before trade unions, church groups, black professional and business groups, and white progressive groups. The American press generally remained silent and did not cover these activities.

A letter-writing campaign had been set up in New York; by October the results of these efforts were clear. Students all over the country were forming defense committees in white and in black colleges. At Fisk University, the University of Chicago, the University of Texas, Wilberforce University, and others "Defense Committees for Dr. Du Bois" were established. They sent letters and telegrams to President Harry S. Truman and to the Development of Justice.

Thus, with tireless work by their lawyers and friends, the officials of the Peace Information Center brought their plight before the world. Contributions for the defense fund came from all over the country in small amounts totaling more than $35,000.

The Doctor's trial was held in Washington, D.C., on November 8, 1951, and it must be kept in mind what the trial was in the eyes of the law. Judge James Mc-Guire, who had been assigned to the case, pointed out that the trial was not to be a question of the beliefs and opinions of Dr. Du Bois and his associates, or a question of whether they had a right to work for peace. It was to be solely a question of whether they were "agents" of a foreign principal or power.

The trial lasted five days. Judge James McGuire was fair and courteous. The prosecution for the United States government headed by F. Kirk Maddrix, former attorney-general of Maryland, seemed to be at best unprepared. But Dr. Du Bois' defense was prepared "to the last comma" and ready for anything.

The prosecution finally placed the outcome of its case on the testimony of O. John Rogge, the very same man who had enlisted Dr. Du Bois' support for the conference on peace two years earlier.[2] Mr. Rogge admitted that he was a member of the Peace Information Center. He said he had attended the World Peace Congress and stated that its basis was not peace. The World Peace Congress, according to Rogge's testimony, was an agent of the Soviet Union.

In his opening statement, Mr. Maddrix had said that the government would not show that there was any "contract of agency" between the World Congress of the Defenders of Peace and the Peace Information Center. Judge McGuire then said: "The responsibility of the government is to prove beyond a reasonable doubt, first of all, the nexus [connection]; and in doing that, you will have to establish, of course, that there was a foreign group. . . ."

Mr. Rogge was permitted to testify that the real purpose of the World Council (formerly Congress) of the Defenders of Peace was to promote the foreign policy of the Soviet Union. And Judge McGuire next asked the prosecution if it intended to show that this organization was an agent of the Soviet Union. Mr. Maddrix would not answer the question directly. Judge McGuire, therefore, said:

> You cannot blow hot and cold. I have got to be advised now as to what you expect to show. . . . You are not, I take it, predicating your case or the theory of your case on the ground that the World Council for Peace was, in effect, the agent of the Soviet Union?

> Mr. Maddrix: We are not making that statement, no.

> The Court: What you do not intend to prove, and I am so advised now, is that you are not going to attempt to prove formally that the activities of the World Council for Peace were the activities of the Soviet Union?

> Mr. Maddrix: I could not state it any better. . . . We do not intend to show that the Committee of the Congress of the World Defenders of Peace was an agent of the Soviet Union.[3]

It became quite clear from this exchange that the testimony of O. John Rogge was meant to smear Russian communism over the case of Dr. Du Bois and his associates and to suggest that the officials of the Peace Information Center were Communists in order to arouse a witch-hunting public against them.

Mr. Marcantonio, Chief Counsel for the defense, began to attack the government's case and argued for a direct acquittal.

The prosecution continued to insist that no connection need be established between the World Council and the Soviet Union because no contractual relationship was required to be shown; "agency" was implied because of the similarity of ideas.

"I contend," said Marcantonio, "and I believe Your Honor has indicated time and time again, that unless connection has been shown, there is no relationship of agency and principal. . . ."

J. Frank Cunningham, a counsel for the government prosecution, pleaded that no connection need be proved:

> You have to go further and show, as your Honor points out, that one was doing it for the other, not necessarily by contract and not necessarily by any agreement at all. The foreign principal may never have heard of the person here, as I have said before. We have to show it was the subjective intent of these people here to disseminate information in the United States, propaganda for and on behalf of, and further the propaganda objectives of the European organization.[4]

The key sentence in the preceding is, "The foreign principal may never have heard of the person here." Judge McGuire asked Mr. Cunningham how it was possible for a person to be guilty of spreading propaganda for a foreign principal if the person had never heard of the principal.

". . . the English language is still the same," said Mr. Marcantonio. "Salt is salt and pepper is pepper. Principal is principal and agent is agent."

Dr. Du Bois and his associates were waiting for the body of evidence—that proof of guilt that the government had for nine months insisted it possessed. This evidence was never presented. The testimony of O. John Rogge was meant to show Dr. Du Bois guilty of treason simply because he held liberal ideas and was not terrified by those holding Communist beliefs.

At last Judge McGuire ruled that the government had failed to prove the allegations laid down in the indictment—that the Peace Information Center and its officers were "agents of a foreign principal." Mr. Marcantonio's motion for acquittal was, therefore, granted.

Judge McGuire said that free thought and tolerance were essential to any society which believed itself to be open and democratic. A society such as America's would have to accept different opinions and philosophies. If it could not, and dissent was stifled, then American society could no longer consider itself free.

At great cost to the United States government and to Dr. Du Bois and his many sympathetic friends across the world, the government had tried him, and he had been found innocent. But what disturbed the Doctor in all this, more than the monetary cost and the mental anguish, was this:

> . . . the certainty that thousands of innocent victims are in jail today because they had neither money, experience nor friends to help them. . . . God only knows how many who were as innocent as I and my colleagues are today in hell. . . . We protect and defend sensational cases where Negroes are involved. But the great mass of arrested or accused black folk have no defense. There is desperate need of nation-wide organizations to oppose this national racket of railroading to jails and chain-gangs the poor, friendless and black.[5]

Dr. Du Bois' defense had cost $35,150; there would have been an additional cost of $10,000 if Marcantonio had not offered his services as chief counsel free of charge. The case was dismissed after five days of trial, having never gone to a jury. And although Dr. Du Bois' innocence was established, he continued to be marked as a criminal. Americans began to act as if he did not exist.

Many other countries, however, wanted the Doctor as their honored guest. The American Intercontinental Peace Conference was to be held in Rio de Janeiro, Brazil. Dr. Du Bois and his wife applied for passports. He had held a passport for fifty-nine years, and his wife, for twenty-four years. On their wedding anni-

versary, February 14, 1952, the Doctor received a
letter from the State Department:

> . . . The Department has given careful consideration
> to your request. However, since it appears that your
> proposed travel would be contrary to the best interest
> of the United States, a passport is not being issued to
> you.
>
> The sum of $9.00 which accompanied your application,
> will be returned to you at a later date. The passport
> which is issued to Mrs. Du Bois on April 5, 1949, is
> being retained in the Department's files.[6]

Dr. Du Bois published the story of his indictment,
trial, and acquittal by the government in the fall of
1952. Entitled *In Battle For Peace,* with comments by
Shirley Graham Du Bois, the book openly gave thanks
to the Communists over the world for their support in
the Doctor's defense.

The publication of *In Battle For Peace,* and Dr. Du
Bois' attack on the government in speech and writing
for its hounding and imprisonment of Communists,
caused the government to watch his activities closely.
His manuscripts and those of his wife were rejected by
many publishing houses. His mail was tampered with;
government agents swarmed through his neighbor-
hood in Brooklyn asking questions of neighbors about
his visitors. Colleges stopped inviting him to lecture.
In short, Dr. Du Bois ceased to be someone every
black American had heard of, for the black press no

longer carried his writings. Always there was the whispered insinuation that because of his age, and not his innocence, the U.S. government had been kind and had acquitted him.

But the old man never ceased his work. He did not cringe or hide. No longer able to travel abroad, he spoke out and wrote whenever he could. The Doctor and his wife adjusted as best they could to their lowered income. How tragic it was that he was no longer the intellectual leader of his people. However, for him, the deepest hurt of all was that black boys and girls would no longer know his name.

CHAPTER 15

D R. DU BOIS, AFTER
1952, was still the distinguished scholar, writer, and
lecturer he had been for years. But the experience of
his indictment, trial, and acquittal released him forever from a view of the black Talented Tenth as a
more humane and self-sacrificing group than any other
among his people. He had for years cherished the
belief that this intellectual, educated group would
honor, teach, and lead less educated and articulate
blacks. The middle class of blacks did not seem to
want this role of leadership. It wanted the money and
affluence which the rest of America possessed; beyond
that, and total integration, it seemed most to want to
be left alone.

Dr. Du Bois was greatly disappointed that the
"Talented Tenth" had not rallied around him during
his indictment and trial; yet he harbored no lasting
resentment. He knew that the accusations against him
were a method used to deprive blacks of strong leader-

ship. In view of recent history, certainly it seems to many that whenever there emerges a strong black leader, either his character or he, himself, is assassinated. The persecution and/or assassination of Malcolm X, Angela Davis, Dr. Martin Luther King, and Dr. Du Bois is believed by many to be the result of a pervasive atmosphere of hate and racial prejudice in America. The expression of this rampant racism is ascribed to the federal goverment's apathy concerning violation of free speech and free thought, liberties guaranteed to the individual by law. If the infringement of these liberties is encouraged by permitting defamation of character, racists are emboldened to pursue their ends by even more extreme tactics, such as violence.

"They have seized on the charge of 'Communism' to silence me," Dr. Du Bois was to charge in his autobiography, "just as they once charged 'Abolition' to shut the mouths of Northerners. And just as today the thrifty are cowed by the threat of revolution."

In the 1950s not only blacks were destroyed in the name of "justice." Ethel and Julius Rosenberg were the subjects of the most sensational spy trial of the century and the first American citizens to be accused of stealing atomic secrets for a foreign power. The evidence in this most complicated case against the Rosenbergs has never been satisfactorily resolved in the minds of many. The student who is interested can find a wealth of books and research documents on the life and work of the Rosenbergs, as well as transcripts of their trial. The facts are simple enough. Julius and Ethel Rosenberg were radical Marxists who in the spring of 1950 were arrested by the Federal Bureau of Investigation and indicted by a federal grand jury under the Espionage Act of 1917 for conspiring to give Russia the secret of the atomic bomb and other national defense secrets. In June 1953 the Rosenbergs were executed by the electric chair in Sing Sing prison.

Dr. W. E. B. Du Bois was one of thousands the world over who had defended the Rosenbergs, convinced that no one "secret" could adequately explain the atomic bomb, which Russia probably had perfect knowledge of in any case. The emotion of the times, which produced the trials of Dr. Du Bois, the Rosenbergs, and others, is made clearer by the following section from *The Betrayers* by Jonathan Root:

> The judge who had given the Rosenbergs the ultimate penalty had blamed them for the Korean War and had twice afterward refused to amend what became an astonishing punitive precedent. Seven times the conviction had been upheld by the U.S. Circuit Court of Appeals and six times the Supreme Court of the United States could find no cause to review the case. Two Presidents of the United States declared the Rosenbergs criminals of the century and refused without a tone of reluctance to spare their lives. Throughout, the moral censure of whole nations was heaped upon the reputation, character and leadership of the United States, whose only rebuttal was the

somewhat patent fact that the Rosenbergs had received the maximum protection of the law, that their execution was neither more nor less than a requirement of that law. . . .

Four times the law had given the Rosenbergs a date with death and three times the law had broken it; even on June 18, hours before they were to die, on the 14th anniversary of their marriage, a U.S. Supreme Court Justice named William O. Douglas had given Julius and Ethel a last incredible stay of execution. Immediately, the Court itself had convened to either uphold or vacate Justice Douglas's action. While the Rosenbergs' lives rested moment by moment on these deliberations, Justice Douglas's career rested in the House office building where a committee of five Congressmen met to draft proceedings aimed at impeaching him for what had been vaguely termed a traitorous act.[1]

During these times Dr. Du Bois lost his place in the leadership of black America. Blacks found it necessary to go along with the current opinion of the times or find themselves unable to work. In 1954 the Supreme Court decision was handed down in the Brown *v.* Board of Education of Topeka case indicating that the "separate but equal" doctrine of the Plessy *v.* Ferguson case was unconstitutional; that, in practice, separate facilities for blacks were inferior to those for whites. Schools could now be desegrated "with all deliberate speed." But fifteen years later, American schools were still segregated. However, in the 1950s it appeared that black Americans were at last receiving redress for centuries of grievances.

The Communist-hunting hysteria of the 1950s was reason enough for the U.S. government to refuse passport privileges to radical thinkers like Dr. Du Bois and the great actor-singer Paul Robeson. Both were confined to America for eight years. Finally, under enormous pressure from foreign countries, the federal government, in a purely administrative decision in 1958, decided that it would be less troublesome to let Mr. Robeson leave the country than to force him to remain. The passport ban on Dr. Du Bois and his wife was also lifted.

The year before, Dr. Du Bois had published the first novel in his projected massive trilogy entitled *The Black Flame*. The first book, called *The Ordeal of Mansart,* covered the years from Reconstruction up to 1916. Focusing on the generations of a family called Mansart, Dr. Du Bois wrote about the meaning of being black in America beginning with the historical period of 1870. The second and third volumes of the trilogy (*Mansart Builds a School,* published in 1959, and *Worlds of Color,* published in 1961) were to continue the Mansart saga through the early 1960s, and the completed trilogy would mirror the life of Dr. Du Bois and the driving struggle and heroism of a whole people.

After the lifting of the passport ban in 1958, Dr. Du Bois sailed for Europe and later traveled extensively in Russia and China to see for himself these Communist countries. The Doctor was greeted by Premier Nikita Khrushchev of the Soviet Union, and in 1959 he received the country's Lenin Peace Prize.

Dr. Du Bois and his wife had intended to go on to Africa, where an "All-African Conference" was taking place. But his difficult and long trip had exhausted him. He entered a Soviet sanitarium situated near Moscow. The physicians there believed the trip to Africa would be too taxing for his frail physique.

The message Dr. Du Bois had prepared for the African conference at Accra, Ghana, was delivered by his wife:

> . . . The whole world, including Capitalist countries, is moving toward Socialism, inevitably, inexorably. You can choose between blocks of military alliance, you can choose between groups of political union, you cannot choose between Socialism and Private Capitalism, because Private ownership of capital is doomed.
>
> But what is Socialism? It is disciplined economy and political organization in which the first duty of a citizen is to serve the state: and the state is not a selected aristocracy, or a group of self-seeking oligarchs who have seized wealth and power. . . . If Africa unites it will be because each part, each nation, each tribe gives up a part of its heritage for the good of the whole. That is what union means; that is what Pan-Africa means. . . .

Dr. Du Bois left the sanitarium near Moscow and traveled to Peking, China, for his ninety-first birthday celebration. He was honored by the Chinese Communist leaders, Mao Tse-tung and Chou En-lai. The speech he gave, in which he pleaded for Chinese and African unity, was broadcast to the world:

> I speak with no authority; no assumption of age nor rank; I hold no position, I have no wealth. One thing alone I own and that is my own soul. Ownership of that I have, even while in my own country for near a century I have been nothing but a 'nigger.' On this basis and this alone I dare speak, I dare advise. . . .

After the long journey, the Doctor and Mrs. Du Bois returned to the United States on the French ship *Liberté*. They had been in China for ten weeks, and the Doctor had made radio broadcasts asserting that repressive conditions existed in the United States. China, by the end of 1949, had a unified central government for the first time since the Revolution of 1912. It was a Communist government, with the socialization of industry and the redistribution of lands. The Chinese Communists had come into the Korean War in 1950, and in 1951 had occupied the country of Tibet. Surely the U.S. government was becoming deeply troubled by the beginning of a military and industrial power represented by the mass of 500 million Chinese people. Little wonder, then, that Dr. Du Bois worried about how he would be received on returning to his own country.

The passports of Dr. Du Bois and his wife were not

taken away from them when they landed. Three months later, however, the State Department demanded them.

Two Americans, Waldo Frank and William Worthy, had sued the State Department for validation of their own passports. Mr. Frank, a writer and lecturer, and Mr. Worthy, correspondent for the *Afro-American* newspaper chain, wanted to visit China. Both cases went to the U.S. Supreme Court for a ruling.

Dr. Du Bois asked that he and his wife be granted a delay in giving their passports until after the Court had made its decision, and his request was granted.[2]

In 1960 Dr. Du Bois was ninety-two years old and rather amazed at his own longevity. He had completed two parts of the three-volume novel, *The Black Flame*. And having always planned his work in detail by the day, week, month, and year, he now found himself uncertain about his future work. He had been seriously ill at the age of fifty. Writing in *Dusk of Dawn* when he was in his early seventies, he gave the impression that he didn't expect he would live very much longer. Yet his life continued, and in his later *Autobiography* he wrote: "Unless by 60 a man has gained possession of enough money to support himself, he faces the distinct possibility of starvation. He is liable to lose his job and to refusal if he seeks another. At 70 he is frowned upon by the church and if he is foolish enough to survive until 90, he is often regarded as a freak."

Beyond the acid humor of these words, there is the feeling of tiredness and a great desire to rest at last. The

Doctor was convinced that in America long life had no significance. One was expected at the age of ninety to be a doddering old fool, if not completely senile. Dr. Du Bois was neither. Furthermore, he saw America as a

> 'Frightened Giant' afraid of the Truth and afraid of Peace. . . . There was a day when the world rightly called Americans honest even if crude; earning their living by hard work; telling the truth no matter whom it hurt; and going to war only in what they believed a just cause after nothing else seemed possible. Today we are lying, stealing, and killing. . . . No nation threatens us. We threaten the world.[3]

In October 1961 Dr. Du Bois, in possession of all of his faculties, joined the Communist party of the United States.

For many, the Doctor's fairly simple act of formally declaring himself a Communist canceled forever his great deeds of the past. A portion of the American public who knew about his activities had been calling him Communist and worse for years, but all his accomplishments became suddenly worthless in the face of America's hysterical fear of the Communist party.[4]

If a serious look is given to Dr. Du Bois' life, one cannot help wondering why he had waited so long to commit himself formally to communism. He had expressed socialist beliefs for half of his life. He openly admired Russia, China, and other Communist countries; and he had been tried as a criminal for his belief in peace. Surely this last was reason enough for him to turn away from a system and country with which he had been consistently at odds.

Whether Dr. Du Bois, on what might have been a bitter impulse, turned his back on America to become a Communist forever, or whether, after deliberate thought he committed himself to the Communist party, is a matter of conjecture which can only serve to confuse what is important.

What is significant is that the Doctor had put into action that which he believed to be right. Earlier in his life he had daringly launched the Niagara Movement to provide black Americans with a protest voice to counteract Booker T. Washington's powerful, well-financed course of moderation. He had moved on to the interracial NAACP and founded *The Crisis,* which was enormously successful in bringing the tenets of black radical thought to a national audience. Finally, he had absorbed Socialist thinking and developed pan-Africanism at a time when world capitalism made darker peoples virtual slaves to imperialism.

By 1939 it was clear to Dr. Du Bois that in the world there existed a new, vital economic system. The system of Marxism was an alternative to capitalism and so-called "free enterprise," which excluded blacks. There was a real country, Russia, which called itself Marxist. In the '30s the idea of social and economic planning was heard everywhere. Therefore, it should have come as no surprise that the Doctor continued to express similar ideas about his planned black economy.

The Russian Revolution and, later, Russian communism hit the world with tremendous force; they affected especially the "backward" peoples—those peoples, as Dr. Du Bois would say, "who did the world's work." Twenty years after the Revolution the capitalist countries strongly feared that communism was the power of the future. Secret Communist agents were imagined to be everywhere. The Peace Information Center and Du Bois were looked upon as a "secret" agent of a foreign power.

For Dr. Du Bois, however, the most extraordinary Communist agent of all time was that vast country, the U.S.S.R.,[5] whose most profound achievement, perhaps, was the intimate feeling it gave to its people—that they by themselves were creating for themselves their own socialist land. And Dr. W. E. B. Du Bois in all likelihood had joined quietly what he hoped would be the future world.

Under the Internal Security Act of 1950 no member of the Communist party could travel outside the United States. In April 1953 the Subversive Activities Control Board, under the provisions of the same act, ordered the Communist party to register. Through appeals to the U.S. Court of Appeals and the U.S. Supreme Court, the validity of the Internal Security Act was successfully challenged for eight years. By 1961 Dr. Du Bois was a member of the Communist party of the United States. The same year, the Supreme Court affirmed the validity of the Internal Security Act, but a ninety-day period was required before the Court's decision could be enforced. Within that period Dr. Du Bois and his wife put their lives in order and prepared to leave the country.

All of the Doctor's personal papers, his unpublished or unfinished works, and his files went to the historian Dr. Herbert Aptheker[6] for safekeeping. Dr. and Mrs. Du Bois then left the country and traveled to Accra, Ghana. President Kwame Nkrumah of Ghana had long been urging "the Father," as he called Dr. Du Bois, "to come home." Furthermore, he wanted Dr. Du Bois to direct the work on the *Encyclopedia Africana,* which the Ghanian government was sponsoring.

Only the Doctor could have known for certain how he felt leaving the United States in 1961. Being a logical and practical man, he must have realized that he would never stand on American soil again. He was ninety-two years old and not likely to live forever. He was also a member of the Communist party, and the Internal Security Act did not allow Communists to enter the country.

Dr. Du Bois traveled to Ghana and didn't look back, although he remained concerned about all that happened in the United States. He took with him the manuscript of his *Autobiography,* which was published in this country in 1968. In its "Postlude" he wrote: "I seek a world where the ideals of communism will triumph—to each according to his need, from each according to his ability. For this I will work as long as I live. And I still live."

In Ghana Dr. Du Bois received all the honors and considerations which had been denied him in his own country. The government built a house for him and his wife. There was a garden and a small hut where the Doctor worked in good weather. Dr. Du Bois prepared information reports for the *Encyclopedia Africana*. The decision was made that African scholars should write the *Encyclopedia* from the body of knowledge about Africa already available, and from that which would now be gathered. White scholars were also utilized to contribute to the research—indeed, scholars all over the world promised their cooperation—but only Africans were to do the actual writing.

Now Dr. Du Bois worked not in isolation but in complete harmony with his surroundings. He was loved and cherished, and in turn, he loved and labored:

> *I lifted up mine eyes to Ghana*
> *And swept the hills with high Hosanna*
> *Above the sun my sight took flight*
> *Till from that pinnacle of light*
> *I saw dropped down this earth of*
>   *crimson, green and gold*
> *Roaring with color, drums and song. . . .*[7]

The Doctor became a Ghanian citizen in 1963. Often he thought about the courageous protest activities of young black men and women in the United States. It was as though they had been listening to what he had been saying for so many years. They gave him renewed hope for the future.

But the old man died. In August 1963 he lay down for the long last time.

In the nation's capital, the actor and playwright Ossie Davis announced the death of Dr. W. E. B. Du Bois just before the multitudes of the March on Washington moved away from the Washington Monument. The human mass of thousands bowed in silence. The young blacks there wondered at the Doctor's dying at a time when they felt themselves most strong.

For they *had* listened to him. They remembered that for more than a quarter of a century he had been the loudest trumpet sound among them; that for most of their own lives he had demanded they accept nothing less than all of the rights of free Americans. His pen had inspired their fathers to offer them no less than courage for the battle and pride enough in themselves to win it.

An ocean lay between the Doctor's death and our lives, but that didn't matter. He was our great man, our keeper, and we were his dream. The distance between us was never far.

NOTES

Chapter One

1. From the poem "The Song of the Smoke" (*The Horizon* magazine, 1899). Reprinted in *Freedomways,* W. E. B. Du Bois Memorial Issue (Vol. 5, No. 1, Winter 1965), p. 92.
2. W. E. B. Du Bois, *The Souls of Black Folk* (1903). Fawcett Publications reprint (1964), pp. 183–184.

Chapter Two

1. A white entertainer, Thomas Rice, made the phrase known throughout the world. Jim Crow was first heard of around 1830 when Rice watched a black singer and dancer performing in an alley. Taking the man's performance and imitating his attire, Rice added to the black man's routine. Rice sang, "Wheel about, turn about, dance jest so—every time I wheel about I shout Jim Crow!"

    Blacks despised the invented character, Jim Crow, but white people laughed and found him hilarious. "Jim Crow" meant for black people all the segregation and discrimination they faced living in America.

Chapter Three

1. *The Autobiography of W. E. B. Du Bois,* published after his death (International Publishers, 1968), Chapter VIII, "I Go

South," pp. 114–115. In the appendices can be found reference notes, a selected bibliography, and a very useful biographical calendar by the editor, Herbert Aptheker.

2. Best described by Dr. Du Bois in *The Souls of Black Folk,* p. 181: "these weird old songs in which the soul of the black slave spoke to men."

   And on p. 189: "Through all the sorrow of the Sorrow Songs there breathes a hope—a faith in the ultimate justice of things. The minor cadences of despair change often to triumph and confidence. Sometimes it is faith in life, sometimes a faith in death, sometimes assurance of boundless justice in some fair world beyond. But whichever it is, the meaning is always clear: that sometime, somewhere, men will judge men by their souls and not by their skins."

3. *Ibid.,* Chapter IV, "Of The Meaning of Progress," p. 64.

Chapter Four

1. The Adams-Onis Treaty of 1819 had fixed the boundary line between the United States and the Spanish Empire. In 1821 Mexico became independent of Spanish rule and inherited the Spanish claim to all territories below the boundary line, from California to the Republic of Texas (1836–1845) and including the Nevada, Utah, Arizona, and New Mexico territories.

   Most of this territory was inhabited by nomadic Indians. American fur-trappers and traders moved in, later followed by farmers. Americans settled in Texas in the 1820s. In 1836 they seceded from Mexico and set up an independent republic. Mexico refused to recognize the independence of Texas. The United States admitted Texas into the Union in 1845 and backed its claim of independence from Mexico. Mexico decided to defend its right to its own territory by force if necessary, for American pioneers now were moving into the Mexican territory of California, also. There followed a war which ended with the Americans victorious. Mexico then surrendered more than half her territories under the Treaty of Guadalupe Hidalgo of 1848.

   The Mexican War has remained controversial to this day. Mexicans have always been angered by this brazen annexation of lands by the United States. Many Americans, like Dr. Du

Bois, believed the war to be a shameful example of our history at its worst.

2. Du Bois, *Autobiography*, p. 149.

Chapter Five

1. MS. from the Du Bois Papers. Somewhat different versions of this diary entry may be found in Du Bois, *Autobiography*, Chapter X, "Europe 1892 to 1894," pp. 170–171; and in *A Documentary History of the Negro People in the United States*, edited by Herbert Aptheker, Vol. 2 (The Citadel Press, 1961), p. 753.
2. Herbert Aptheker, "Du Bois as Historian," *Negro History Bulletin* (Vol. 32, No. 4, April 1969), Footnote 22, p. 15.
3. W. E. B. Du Bois, *The Philadelphia Negro: A Social Study* (1899). Schocken Books reprint (1967), p. 309.
4. *Ibid.*, p. 352.

Chapter Six

1. *Civil Rights and the American Negro: A Documentary History*, edited by Albert P. Blaustein and Robert L. Zangrando (Washington Square Press, 1968), Document 62, "Speech of Senator Benjamin R. Tillman," pp. 320–321.
2. Du Bois, *Autobiography*, p. 222.

Chapter Seven

1. Booker T. Washington, *Up from Slavery* (1901). Avon Library reprint (in *Three Negro Classics*, 1965), pp. 148–149. Further autobiographical reading: *The Story of My Life and Work* (Hertel, Jenkins and Co., 1900).
2. Ridgely Torrence, *The Story of John Hope* (The Macmillan Company, 1948), pp. 114–115.
3. Washington, *Up from Slavery*, p. 155.
4. Du Bois, *The Souls of Black Folk*, pp. 16–17.
5. August Meir, "Booker T. Washington and the Negro Press," *Journal of Negro History* (Vol. 38, January 1953), p. 71.

Chapter Eight

1. Aptheker, *A Documentary History of the Negro People*, Vol. 2, "Niagara Address of 1906" by W. E. B. Du Bois, p. 909.
2. *Ibid.*, "Mr. Barber's Letter to the New York *World*," pp. 866–867.
3. W. E. B. Du Bois, *Darkwater* (1920). Schocken Books reprint (1969), "A Litany at Atlanta," p. 26.
4. Du Bois, *Autobiography*, p. 253.
5. Aptheker, *A Documentary History of the Negro People*, Vol. 2, "The National Negro Committee on Mr. Washington, 1910," p. 884.

Chapter Nine

1. Aptheker, *A Documentary History of the Negro People*, Vol. 2, "Negro Anti-Republicanism, 1908," pp. 857–858.
2. *Negro Protest Thought in the Twentieth Century*, edited by Francis L. Broderick and August Meier (The Bobbs-Merrill Company, Inc., 1965), "Socialist of the Path" by W. E. B. Du Bois, p. 53.
3. This document is reprinted in its entirety in Blaustein and Zangrando, *Civil Rights and the American Negro*, "A French Directive," pp. 335–336.
4. William L. Katz, *Eyewitness: The Negro in American History* (Pitman Publishing Corporation, 1967), p. 394.

Chapter Ten

1. Blaustein and Zangrando, *Civil Rights and the American Negro*, "The Tenth Annual Report of the NAACP for the Year 1919," pp. 338–339.
2. W. E. B. Du Bois, *Dusk of Dawn: An Essay Toward an Autobiography of a Race Concept* (1940). Schocken Books reprint (1968), pp. 284–285.
3. Eleanor Desverney Sinnette, "The Brownies' Book," *Freedomways*, Du Bois Memorial Issue, p. 138.
4. Elliott M. Rudwick, *W. E. B. Du Bois: Propagandist of the Negro Protest* (Atheneum Publishers, 1968), p. 242.

Chapter Eleven

1. Du Bois, *Autobiography*, p. 321. Pages 312–319 give a thorough explanation of Dr. Du Bois' extraordinary plan of social studies for Negro colleges and graduate schools. On page 312 is given the purpose of college, in the Doctor's view: "The college today, however, must do more—far more—than prepare men for jobs at present in demand and socially needful. The college must anticipate the future needs of the community and prepare education to meet them."

Chapter Twelve

1. The Fourth Pan-African Congress met in London and Lisbon in 1923; the Fifth, in New York in 1927.
2. Richard B. Moore, "Du Bois and Pan Africa," *Freedomways,* Du Bois Memorial Issue, p. 184.
3. W. E. B. Du Bois, with comment by Shirley Graham, *In Battle for Peace: The Story of My Eighty-third Birthday* (Masses & Mainstream, 1952), p. 24.
4. *Ibid.,* p. 27.
5. *Ibid.,* p. 28.
6. *Ibid.,* p. 37.
7. Francis L. Broderick, *W. E. B. Du Bois: Negro Leader in a Time of Crisis* (Stanford University Press, 1959), pp. 209–210.

Chapter Thirteen

1. Du Bois, *In Battle for Peace,* p. 52.

Chapter Fourteen

1. Du Bois, *In Battle for Peace,* p. 82.
2. The liberal O. John Rogge became an ex-Progressive with the defeat of the Progressive party presidential candidate, Henry Wallace, in 1948. He further trimmed his left-wing sails as cold-war politics hurt his law practice. Rogge became an agent of the Yugoslav Mission in New York at the time Yugoslavia broke

with the Soviet Union on ideological grounds. Thereafter, Rogge became increasingly critical of Russian communism.

3. Du Bois, *In Battle for Peace*, p. 130.
4. *Ibid.*, p. 143.
5. *Ibid.*, p. 153.
6. *Ibid.*, p. 192.

Chapter Fifteen

1. Jonathan Root, *The Betrayers: The Rosenberg Case—a Reappraisal of an American Crisis* (Coward-McCann, Inc., 1963), pp. 15–16.
2. Du Bois, *Autobiography,* Reference Note 17, pp. 429–430.
3. *Ibid.*, p. 415.
4. "Hysterical" in that the Communist party polled only 48,600 votes in the 1940 presidential election out of nearly 49 million votes cast. The Party had no ticket of its own in the 1944 and 1948 elections.
5. The U.S.S.R., the Union of Soviet Socialist Republics, was established in 1922. Its first four members were the Russian Soviet Federated Socialist Republic, the Ukrainian Soviet Socialist Republic, the White Russian Soviet Socialist Republic, and the Transcaucasian Socialist Federal Soviet Republic. Geographically, this new Union replaced the Russian Empire; the name "Russia" was no longer officially used.
6. See the Du Bois Memorial Issue of *Freedomways,* "Some Unpublished Writings of W. E. B. Du Bois," compiled and presented by Herbert Aptheker, p. 103. Dr. Aptheker, the literary executor of the Du Bois Papers, states that "This enormous collection dates from the late 1870s and terminates in the 1960s; the separate items must certainly number in the hundreds of thousands."
7. From the poem, "Ghana Calls," subtitled, "To Osagyefo Kwame Nkrumah" (*Freedomways,* 1962). Reprinted in Du Bois Memorial Issue, p. 99.

BIBLIOGRAPHY

The books, essays, articles, and poems cited in the notes and in the section of the bibliography listing writings by W. E. B. Du Bois are a small part of the vast amount of works produced by Dr. Du Bois. A complete bibliography might run more than one hundred pages. The selected bibliography Dr. Herbert Aptheker added to *The Autobiography of W. E. B. Du Bois* and Ernest Kaiser's bibliography in *Freedomways,* Winter 1965, are excellent sources.

The works by Du Bois in the following list are available through libraries and bookstores.

Writings by W. E. B. Du Bois

The Suppression of the African Slave Trade to the United States of America, 1638–1870. Harvard Historical Series, No. 1. New York: Longmans, Green, 1896. Reprinted, New York: Russell & Russell, Inc., 1965.

The Philadelphia Negro: A Social Study. Philadelphia: University of Pennsylvania Press, 1899. Reprinted, New York: B. Blom, 1967. New York: Schocken Books, Inc., 1967.

The Souls of Black Folk: Essays and Sketches. Chicago: A. C. McClurg and Co., 1903. Reprinted, New York: Fawcett World Library, 1964.

John Brown. Philadelphia: George W. Jacobs and Co., 1909. Reprinted, New York: International Publishers, 1962.

The Quest of the Silver Fleece. Chicago: A. C. McClurg and Co., 1911.

The Negro. Home University Library of Knowledge, XCI. New York: Henry Holt & Company, 1915.

Darkwater: The Twentieth Century Completion of Uncle Tom's Cabin. Washington: A. Jenkins Co., 1920. Reprinted, New York: Harcourt,

Brace & Howe (with subtitle *Voices from Within the Veil*), 1930; New York: Schocken Books, Inc., 1969.

The Gift of Black Folk: Negroes in the Making of America. Boston: Stratford Co., 1924.

Dark Princess: A Romance. New York: Harcourt, Brace & Company, 1928.

Black Reconstruction in America, 1860–1880. New York: Harcourt, Brace & Company, 1935. Reprinted, New York: Meridian Books, 1964.

Dusk of Dawn: An Essay Toward an Autobiography of a Race Concept. New York: Harcourt, Brace & Company, 1940. Reprinted, New York: Schocken Books, 1968.

The World and Africa: An Inquiry into the Part which Africa has Played in World History. New York: The Viking Press, 1947. Reprinted, New York: International Publishers, 1965.

Color and Democracy. New York: Harcourt, Brace & Company, 1945.

In Battle For Peace: The Story of my Eighty-third Birthday. With comment by Shirley Graham. New York: Masses & Mainstream, 1952.

The Black Flame—A Trilogy: The Ordeal of Mansart, 1957; *Mansart Builds A School,* 1959; *Worlds of Color,* 1961. New York: Mainstream Publishers.

A Recorded Autobiography. New York: Folkways Records, Inc., 1961.

"The Negro People and the United States." *Freedomways,* Vol. I, No. 1 (Spring 1961), pp. 11–19.

An ABC of Color: Selections from Over a Half Century of the Writings of W. E. B. Du Bois. Berlin, German Democratic Republic: Seven Seas Publishers, 1963.

"Selected Poems of W. E. B. Du Bois," presented by Shirley Graham Du Bois. *Freedomways,* W. E. B. Du Bois Memorial Issue, Vol. V, No. 1 (Winter 1965), pp. 88–102.

"Some Unpublished Writings of W. E. B. Du Bois," compiled and presented by Herbert Aptheker. *Freedomways,* W. E. B. Du Bois Memorial Issue, Vol. V, No. 1 (Winter 1965), pp. 103–128.

The Autobiography of W. E. B. Du Bois: A Soliloquy on Viewing My Life from the Last Decade of Its First Century. Edited by Herbert Aptheker. New York: International Publishers, 1968.

Selected Sources

APTHEKER, HERBERT, *A Documentary History of the Negro People in the United States.* Vol. 2, *From the Reconstruction Era to 1910.* New York: The Citadel Press, 1961.

——— "Du Bois as Historian." *Negro History Bulletin,* Vol. 32, No. 4 (April 1969), pp. 6–16.

—— *Toward Negro Freedom*. New York: New Century Publishers, 1956.

BERNSTEIN, BARTON J., and MATUSOW, ALLEN J., editors, *The Truman Administration: A Documentary History*. New York: Harper & Row, Publishers, 1966.

BLAUSTEIN, ALBERT P., and ZANGRANDO, ROBERT L., editors, *Civil Rights and the American Negro: A Documentary History*. New York: Washington Square Press, 1968.

BOND, HORACE MANN, *et al.*, "The Legacy of W. E. B. Du Bois." *Freedomways*, W. E. B. Du Bois Memorial Issue, Vol. V, No. 1 (Winter 1965), pp. 16–40.

BONTEMPS, ARNA, and CONROY, JACK, *Anyplace but Here*. New York: Hill & Wang, Inc., 1966.

BRODERICK, FRANCIS L., *W. E. B. Du Bois, Negro Leader in a Time of Crisis*. Stanford: Stanford University Press, 1959.

—— and MEIER, AUGUST, editors, *Negro Protest Thought in the Twentieth Century*. New York: The Bobbs-Merrill Company, Inc., 1965.

BROWN, ROSCOE C., JR., and PLOSKI, HARRY A., editors, *The Negro Almanac*. New York: Bellwether Publishing Company, Inc., 1966.

BUTCHER, MARGARET JUST, *The Negro In American Culture* (based on materials left by Alain Locke). New York: Alfred A. Knopf, Inc., 1956.

CHAFFEE, M. L., "William E. B. Du Bois' Concept of the Racial Problem in the United States." *Journal of Negro History*, Vol. XLI (July 1956), pp. 241–258.

CLARKE, JOHN HENRIK, editor, *Harlem, U.S.A.: The Story of a City Within a City*. Berlin, German Democratic Republic: Seven Seas Publishers, 1964.

DUBERMAN, MARTIN, "Du Bois as Prophet." *New Republic*, Vol. CLVIII (March 23, 1968), pp. 36–39.

EMANUEL, JAMES A., and GROSS, THEODORE L., editors, *Dark Symphony: Negro Literature in America*. New York: The Free Press, 1968.

FERGUSON, BLANCHE E., *Countee Cullen and the Negro Renaissance*. New York: Dodd, Mead & Co., 1966.

FOX, STEPHEN R., *The Guardian of Boston: William Monroe Trotter*. New York: Atheneum Publishers, 1970.

FRANKLIN, JOHN HOPE, and STARR, ISIDORE, editors, *The Negro In Twentieth Century America: A Reader on the Struggle for Civil Rights.* New York: Vintage Books, 1967.

GOLDBERG, HARVEY, editor, *American Radicals: Some Problems and Personalities.* New York: Monthly Review Press, 1969.

HOFSTADTER, RICHARD, *The Age of Reform: From Bryan to F.D.R.* New York: Alfred A. Knopf, Inc., 1955.

———— *The Paranoid Style in American Politics.* New York: Alfred A. Knopf, Inc., 1965.

JOHNSON, JAMES WELDON, *Black Manhattan.* New York: Alfred A. Knopf, Inc., 1930. New York: Atheneum Publishers, 1968.

KAISER, ERNEST, "A Selected Bibliography of the Published Writings of W. E. B. Du Bois." *Freedomways,* W. E. B. Du Bois Memorial Issue, Vol. V, No. 1 (Winter 1965) pp. 207–213.

KATZ, WILLIAM L., *Eyewitness: The Negro in American History.* New York: Pitman Publishing Corporation, 1967.

LOCKE, ALAIN, editor, *The New Negro.* New York: Albert & Charles Boni, Inc., 1925. Reprinted, New York: Atheneum Publishers, 1968.

LOGAN, RAYFORD W., *The Negro in American Life and Thought: The Nadir, 1877–1901.* New York: Dial Press, 1954. 2nd edition: *The Betrayal of the Negro: From Rutherford B. Hayes to Woodrow Wilson.* New York: Collier Books, 1965.

MARCANTONIO, VITO, *I Vote My Conscience: Debates, Speeches and Writings.* New York: The Vito Marcantonio Memorial, 1956.

MEIER, AUGUST, *Negro Thought in America, 1880–1915.* Ann Arbor: University of Michigan Press, 1963.

———— and MELTZER, MILTON, *Time of Trial, Time of Hope: The Negro in America 1919–1941.* New York: Doubleday & Company, Inc. (Zenith Books), 1966.

———— and RUDWICK, ELLIOTT, editors, *The Making of Black America.* Vol. 2, *The Black Community in Modern America.* New York: Atheneum Publishers, 1969.

MYRDAL, GUNNAR, *An American Dilemma.* New York: Harper & Row, Publishers, 1962.

ROBESON, PAUL, *Here I Stand.* New York: Othello Associates, 1958.

ROOT, JONATHAN, *The Betrayers: The Rosenberg Case—a Reappraisal of an American Crisis.* New York: Coward-McCann, Inc., 1963.

STERLING, DOROTHY, and QUARLES, BENJAMIN, *Lift Every Voice: The Lives of Booker T. Washington, W. E. B. Du Bois, Mary Church Terrell, and James Weldon Johnson.* New York: Doubleday & Company, 1965.

RUDWICK, ELLIOTT M., *W. E. B. Du Bois: Propagandist of the Negro Protest.* New York: Atheneum Publishers, 1968.

SALK, ERWIN A., editor, *A Layman's Guide to Negro History.* Chicago: Quadrangle Books, 1966.

SCHLESINGER, ARTHUR MEIER, *The Rise of Modern America: 1865–1951.* New York: The Macmillan Company, 1951.

WALLING, WILLIAM ENGLISH, *Socialism as It Is.* New York: The Macmillan Company, 1912.

WASHINGTON, BOOKER T., *Up from Slavery.* Included in *Three Negro Classics,* edited by John Hope Franklin. New York: Avon paperback, 1965.

INDEX